How Does Change Happen?

Published by 404 Ink Limited
www.404Ink.com
hello@404ink.com

Please note: Some references include URLs which may change or be unavailable after publication of this book. All references within endnotes were accessible and accurate as of April 2025 but may experience link rot from there on in.

Editing: Laura Jones-Rivera
Proofreading: Heather McDaid
Typesetting: Laura Jones-Rivera
Cover design: Luke Bird
Co-founders and publishers of 404 Ink:
Heather McDaid & Laura Jones-Rivera

Print ISBN: 978-1-916637-12-2
Ebook ISBN: 978-1-916637-13-9

EU GPSR Authorised Representative
LOGOS EUROPE, 9 rue Nicolas Poussin,
17000, LA ROCHELLE, France
E-mail: Contact@logoseurope.eu

Printed and bound in Great Britain by Clays Ltd, Elcograf S.p.A.

MIX
Paper | Supporting
responsible forestry
FSC
www.fsc.org
FSC® C018072

How Does Change Happen?

Scenes From the Frontlines of Activism

Sam Gonçalves

Inklings

Contents

Para Stella, que entendia de mudanças.

Introduction
Umbrella Man

Everything changed when bullets flew over the crowd. The target was John F. Kennedy, who had been elected President of the United States only three years earlier in 1960. His driver sped away as the shots rained down, but it was too late.

The assassination gathered the attention of conspiracy theorists for decades, which I personally find as fascinating as the event itself. They picked apart every detail of that ill-fated Friday in Dallas: how many shooters were at the scene, how many bullets had been fired, and the possible involvement of any or all of the CIA, the Mafia, Cuba, Soviet Union or – my personal favourite – a secret service agent who some believed simply lost his balance and accidentally killed the President.[1]

A few years ago, I nursed a small obsession over the JFK assassination. A customary rite of passage for my culture – men in their thirties. I was particularly inter-ested in the marginal characters. The bystanders whose world was upended. My research led me to an odd detail about the event, an under-discussed mystery in the margins. Unmistakably there in the crowd, right where the shooting started, stood a man with an umbrella. An open umbrella on a sunny day. You can see him wearing a dark suit in the grainy video footage. He stands out from the crowd in the Texas heat. For years, 'Umbrella Man' became the source of endless speculation.[2] An anachro-nistic detail that felt too juicy to be a coincidence. Too odd to ignore. A public search ensued, leading to congres-sional hearings where sketches were presented outlining how someone might be able to adapt an umbrella into a functioning gun.

As interest grew, Umbrella Man identified himself as Louie Steven Witt, a life insurance salesman. He testified that he was at the site of the assassination to protest Joseph Kennedy Sr., JFK's father, for his support of Neville Chamberlain, the British Prime Minister infamous for his soft stance on Adolf Hitler just before the Second World War.

Did you follow that? Witt was protesting JFK's father's friend's association, twenty-four years after the fact. His convoluted way of staging this protest was to hold up a black umbrella, an item often associated as Chamberlain's accessory of choice.

It just so happens he decided to do this action at the time and location where the history of his country would change indefinitely. Years later, Witt testified to congress. 'I think if the Guinness Book of World Records had a category for people who were at the wrong place at the wrong time, doing the wrong thing, I would be No. 1.'[3]

There's something about Louie that I find relatable. Perhaps it's the feeling of complete helplessness when it comes to having a positive impact in the world. I am writing this a few weeks after Trump's 2024 re-election, which seems to have been met with less of the fightback that occurred in 2016 and more of a collective sigh of despair. Most political parties that pitch themselves as alternatives to this global move to the right seem completely ineffective or morally bankrupt. We are watching the world burn through minute-by-minute updates on the three or four screens that surround us at all times. The same apps that dole out doom offer us the option to do something about it: petitions, hashtags, Canva-designed Instagram posts. The signifiers of protest have become palatable enough to be seen as a nice hobby or to sell Pepsi.[4] It doesn't take long to find advertising for the most mundane household items that call on the viewer to 'join the movement', and yet, despite these newly accessible reins of power, change never seemed so far from our control. We are left feeling like we're holding an umbrella on a sunny day, watching the world fall apart while our cause is forgotten by history.

Resistance can often feel impotent and trite, but to lose hope in it is a luxury the ruling classes would love for us to indulge. In the last few decades, neoliberalism has eroded structures that once fostered community and security in the last few decades – public services, secure wage labour, trade unions, local neighbourhoods, to name a few.[5] With fewer reliable foundations from which communities can be built, we become increasingly isolated. Work is uncertain. Housing is uncertain. Healthcare is uncertain. While some of the issues facing the world today seem monumental, there's a deep despair in knowing that we're facing them alone.

As the system attempts to salt the earth from where community might grow, it tries to convince us we can achieve anything we set our minds to. All we have to do is pick ourselves up by our bootstraps, find a side hustle, set up a source of passive income. When our perspectives on making change are influenced by this growing, state-sanctioned smog of individualism, we end up talking about activism as a branch of personal responsibility. We focus on self-improvement, voting and recycling – all good and important things that alone will never be a reliable transformational force in society. It is not surprising that in an isolated and atomised world, changing anything systemic has become an act of the personal, the self.

In *If We Burn*, Vicent Bevins discusses protests through the 2010s, a time that saw more direct action on the streets globally than any previous decade.[6] One of the foundational questions that he tackles is why so many of those movements failed, or seemed to lead to completely different outcomes than originally hoped. Many of his interviewees touch on the dangers of 'do somethingism',[7] or the fallacy that as long as you get out there and make your voice heard, everything will be okay. As we know by now, it won't.

How Does Change Happen? was born from a frustration I often find myself in, the space between longing for meaningful social change and the action required, because despite all of these structural hurdles, giving up on hope is the refuge of the ultra-rich.

In his book *Survival of the Richest*, Douglas Rushkoff recounts being invited by a group of billionaire survivalists to discuss the end of civilisation. He expected the conversation would be an exploration of some of the most urgent issues facing humanity and how this powerful group could use their abundant resources to prevent it. Instead, the men were interested in the answer to one question, which boiled down to the essence of: 'If civilisation collapses, how do I keep my employees loyal to me?'[8]

Over the last couple of years, I asked just about everyone I met 'how does change happen?' so I could engage with the grimness of the world in different terms. Even when I did interviews for unrelated projects, I snuck the question in. Consistently, this would be met with an eyeroll and an annoyed sigh, sometimes with a number of clarifying questions, but after the initial frustration there was a visible shift where interviewees got something off their chest. They would dissect their motivations, excavate the meagre signs of hope that kept them going. Some of them would look at me with a conspiratorial tone and share formative moments in their lives. In the beginning I was apologetic about the vagueness of the question but, eventually, it was a pleasure to throw it out in the simplest terms and watch what happened.

Some of the answers gave me glimpses of what could happen when we don't see activism as just another stop on the journey of self-improvement, or dimension for a personal brand. I spent a year meeting organisers who have inspired me with their brilliant strategic thinking, surprising creativity and life-altering sacrifice.

The title of this book ends with a question mark, because what I hope to achieve in the following chapters is not a finite, scholarly textbook answer, or a step by step roadmap, but instead a wrestling with the question through communities who are neck-deep in the struggle of changing the world around them.

I have often found that meaningful experiences of learning come through stories. A lot of the interviewees I met emotionally process their activism through stories too. They discuss strategy through tales of conflict. They plan action by re-telling anecdotes of past success.

They commiserate through shared accounts of what didn't work so well. So, in *How Does Change Happen?*, I decided to explore theories of change by translating, as historian Hayden White writes in *The Content of the Form*, 'knowing into telling'.[9]

For each chapter, I met with a number of activists in a given area and explored questions around change. Throughout, I will be making reference to relevant news and literature in order to provide some context, but at its core, what you will find in the coming pages is my attempt to represent conversations with individuals as I experienced them.

The following is a journey through stories of change, and the communities powering them.

Chapter 1
Educate

My first conversation with Pinar Aksu happened in the Summer of 2024. We picked up some coffees and walked over to Glasgow's Kelvingrove Park to find a bench. She is a community organiser and educator, involved in several campaigns and deeply engaged with key movements in the city and beyond.

It was one of those days when you can't quite tell if it's warm or if you have been in Scotland long enough for your concept of 'cold' to be skewed. Either way, we were going to talk about the hostile environment in the UK for refugees, asylum seekers and immigrants, as well as some of the organising that has been done to combat it – a tough topic to discuss comprehensively. In the first half of the 2020s alone, you can talk about immigration detention centres, dawn raids, low quality housing, and an openly racist atmosphere in the national media. Key legislation was passed, like the Nationality and Borders Act, the Illegal Migration Act, the Safety of Rwanda Act, all making life significantly harder for many people.

An incident at Glasgow's Park Inn Hotel in June 2020 was a particular low point for Pinar, when an asylum seeker was shot dead by police after stabbing six individuals.[1] 'I would have assumed after [Park Inn] they would have maybe stopped using hotels or they would have changed something but no, they didn't.'[2]

The use of hotels to house asylum seekers has been criticised by campaigners due to the isolation, poverty and poor mental health it generates.[3] They argue asylum seekers should be housed in communities, where they can integrate in 'dignified, safe, habitable, and fit for purpose accommodations.'[4] Still, nothing's changed.

It all contributes to a paralysing sense that things could not possibly get better, she continued. 'People feel defeated because we are like, *Okay what's the worst that could happen that's going to make things U-turn?* Then worse things happen and things do not change.'

It's not difficult to lose any sense of hope in a situation like this. 'Sometimes I'm like, what's the point?' Pinar explained, 'because the laws are getting worse and worse.'

Governments May Use Different Words

Pinar came to Scotland from Turkey when she was eight years old. When you move countries at that age, you often don't understand what is going on but Pinar has positive memories of her school and the community around her. At fourteen, she was taken to an immigration detention centre along with her parents and siblings.

Pinar's community rallied around her family, gaining support from politicians, charities and campaign groups. Their efforts resulted in a positive outcome. After more than two months in detention, her family were one of the few to be released. Pinar, being the eldest of the siblings, became the translator for her parents. She had a front seat to the impact a grassroots campaign could have.

In a piece for the End the Immigration Detention of Children campaign, she wrote, 'I don't see any difference between a detention centre and a prison. Governments may use different words to make these policies sound acceptable, however it is the same as I was being deprived of my liberty without cause. Our rights as citizens were taken away. As a child at the time, I saw many things that no child should see.'[5]

She didn't always want to be organising around these issues. Pinar was going to study chemical engineering at university, but at a certain point realised she might feel more at home pursuing a place in community development after spending her whole life witnessing campaigns and activists first hand. 'I think all these things added lots of experience and I was able to see different issues in different communities and how communities come together, the importance of dialogue, not judging one another.'

Currently, as the Human Rights Advocacy Coordinator for Maryhill Integration Network, Pinar is part of a number of campaigns for the rights of asylum seekers including the Right to Vote campaign, advocating for asylum seekers to be able to vote on Scottish elections[6] and the Our Grades Not Visas campaign, which identified the barriers for refugees to access further education.[7] Both were clear and recent successes. Then there is the on-going Right to Work campaign, advocating for asylum seekers to be granted permission to find employment – which they are currently not allowed to do,[8] and the End Hotel Detention campaign, backing community-based residential accommodation for asylum seekers.[9]

Sat on the park bench, I was keen to ask her about two things that stick out to me about these campaigns. On the one hand, they seem to be moving fast. In the last few years there have been many legislative wins that had a direct impact on people's lives. In early 2024, a campaign for free bus travel for asylum seekers received a positive response from the Government and looked like it would be implemented rapidly. On the other hand, the barrier to these campaigns is the immigration policy in the UK, the aforementioned 'hostile environment'. Can the monumental weight of anti-immigration media coverage, public sentiment and policy ever be shifted?

Pinar seemed to agree with these two elements of the organising she's involved in. One of the main reasons it can be so difficult to effectively bring about change around this issue, she believes, is that the racism and hostility are deeply structural. They imbue the system. Even in administrations that are not openly aggressive in their discourse.

Her point seems to bear out within that very same summer in 2024. After fourteen years of a Conservative government that was not only aggressive in the policies but used immigration as a regular rhetorical tool, Labour came into power with a campaign accusing the incumbents of being too 'liberal' on immigration.[10] While they eventually scrapped the Rwanda deportation plan,[11] the new government soon committed to reopening Immigration Detention Centres that were closed.[12]

Pinar uses the example of the Right to Work campaign. It has been going for over five years, she has seen it all, been part of it for the whole time and nothing has changed. Recently, at a strategy meeting, one of the campaigners voiced their frustration saying, 'What's the point? I still can't work, and this is so stressful for me.'

Pinar described responding to the sentiment. 'I go speechless and I'm like, *You're right. It's frustrating, isn't it?* So, I'm not going to go and lie to you and say, *No, don't be silly. It's going to be fine.* It's not going to be fine. Things are probably going to get worse, but we need to talk about what we are going to do when things are going to get worse.'

It's a difficult reality to take in, especially after years of campaigning, but accepting that truth and reflecting on the circumstances as they are is often the way through. As disputes like Right to Work and Free Bus Travel get more protracted, and decision makers more impenetrable, the ability to look at the issue from new angles is essential. Pinar believes there is a way to make it past these challenges: 'We must think creatively about how we reflect the truth.' In these moments that feel like dead ends, education becomes a vital tool.

Rehearsal of Revolution

Education is a key element of Pinar's work. An example of it can be found in the cards Pinar produced when the Rwanda Bill came into effect. On these cards was information for refugees and asylum seekers about what to do if they got detained, including lawyer details, as their phones are often taken away by the authorities. This kind of resource is necessary, but uncomfortable. 'It's such a bad process that the state violence is so incredible that we have to create a forum for people who might be detained,' Pinar explained.

But there is a deeper understanding of education that often gets missed from these kinds of initiatives. In Pinar's definition, it is about the way a community approaches the reality of their experience, 'creative ways to change the narrative'. The approach is made up of two steps; first, an honest and informed appraisal of where things are at and a willingness to confront losses and failures of strategy; second, stemming from that appraisal, creatively exploring a way forward. These steps can be done through, for example, the addition of a game to what would otherwise be a routine strategy meeting, but, for the most part, in Pinar's work, they come together best through theatre.

When we discuss politics and theatre, we have to talk about Augusto Boal, the Brazilian educator, theatre practitioner and activist, responsible for developing a critically engaged form of theatre he labelled Theatre of the Oppressed. The political approach to dramaturgy would get participants to enact scenes about the problems they were facing as a community and find a way forward together.[13] The audience is an involved part of the story, not just spectators. 'Perhaps the theatre is not revolutionary in itself,' he writes in 1985's *Theatre of the Oppressed*, 'but it is surely a rehearsal for the revolution!'[14]

Boal is an important figure to Pinar. Coincidentally, they were both attracted to chemical engineering early in life, but then shifted their focus to theatre and activism. She has been a Theatre of the Oppressed practitioner for years. I asked her to give me an example of what this engagement may look like in practice and she told me about a particular evening in October 2024.

She brought together a group of sixty-five people, including immigration lawyers, refugee organisations, academics and artists. The group was also made up of many people who are currently in the asylum process. Once everyone was ready, a play began – a series of scenes, written and performed by Pinar and her colleagues, demonstrating common issues experienced by asylum seekers. Once the play was finished, Pinar asked the audience about the barriers they observed in those scenes. A handful of moments are identified and then it is time for everyone to break into groups and discuss what kind of legislation would improve the situation.

As the suggestions were made, the scenes were re-enacted – this time with the alterations generated in the groups. At every turn, Pinar asked, 'Did that change anything?' Ideas get tested. Policies are honed.

At this point, there is a group to the side that has not yet been mentioned – the policy chamber. They are made up of a lawyer, a policy maker and an activist who have been briefed on their role beforehand. Their job was to now look at all the legislation proposed and pick twelve of the best ones. Eventually, they present the twelve back to the audience. Then it's time for a vote. Everyone gets a green card and a red card. The group selects three of the policies that worked best and should be a priority. Now, it is the responsibility of the attendees to take these policies forward, which will eventually make up the bare bones of a new campaign.

What is born out of the procedure of bringing people into a room who might otherwise rarely get a chance to meet becomes a collaborative effort. A piece of policy that takes into account both the lived experience of the people who it will affect the most, as well as the collective knowledge of individuals who see different angles of it.

Creativity, dialogue, and collaboration – these three ingredients form this collective's approach to education, which leads to an understanding of oppression and imagining of ways to overcome it. Despite the immovable object of the hostile environment, these tools seem to have consistent success in creating campaigns that make change happen.

Before I finished my conversation with Pinar, we spoke again about the campaign fighting to provide free bus transport for asylum seekers, which was all but a confirmed success at this point.[15] This policy has the potential to meaningfully change the lives of anyone seeking asylum in Scotland as asylum seekers are, by law, blocked from employment and receive meagre weekly stipends. Free bus travel means access to healthcare, nature, solicitor appointments, volunteering and more. It's a change in policy that goes a long way towards fighting the crushing isolation many asylum seekers face and avoiding anyone having to choose between transport and food.[16] It's the kind of direct, achievable, transformational change that happens through a committed campaign.

Pinar and I said our goodbyes. As I walked away I thought about the free bus travel campaign. The carefully strategised and timely win seemed like the perfect answer to the question of how we can stay hopeful against such unlikely odds.

Little did I know that it would soon fall apart.

Protagonism of the Masses

In Boal's home country, this collaborative form of education has been used as a tool for mass movements for decades.

In May 2024, massive floods hit the southern state of Rio Grande do Sul in Brazil. The torrential rain started at the end of April, but intensified over an entire month. The videos were apocalyptic; public markets half covered in water, a bridge swept away, families calling out for rescue on their roofs, a woman being dragged by the current. At its highest, the water level reached 17.5ft. The tragedy claimed 179 lives and 600,000 people evacuated their homes.[17]

On May 21st, I spoke to Edgar Kolling through a video call. With a welcoming demeanour and strong southern accent (which in Brazil means a rolling of the tongue on the Rs), he performed the role of a host and made sure I was comfortable and doing well. When I finally got a chance to cut in and ask about how he is doing as the flood devastates his home state, I got good news. Edgar had been safe and mostly unaffected. At one point he was 'surrounded by water'[18] but everything was okay.

Activism around land and home are part of the reason we were on this call. Edgar has been an activist and educator, part of Brazil's Landless Workers' Movement (Movimento Dos Trabalhadores Rurais Sem Terra – MST), since 1986. Founded in 1984, the mass movement organises rural workers with the goal of national land reform. According to an OXFAM study, 45% of all rural areas in Brazil are owned by less than 1% of property owners.[19] This is the exact type of inequality MST was created to fight.

According to Brazil's Federal Constitution, land that does not serve a social function can be expropriated.[20] MST, then, occupies land that has often been abandoned or causes environmental harm to its surroundings. The owner is permitted to file suit for repossession as long as he can prove that the land does in fact follow a social function. Once that land is won by the movement it becomes, in the eyes of the law, an assentamento, housing families who live off the land. As of 2016 there were around 2,000 of these permanent settlements, and over 1.5 million members.[21] After 40 years of this struggle, MST is now in 24 of 26 Brazilian states and is the largest producer of organic food in Brazil.[22]

The very first MST occupation was in Rio Grande do Sul.[23] Since then, they have grown exponentially as a movement across the country. Its goals are personal to Edgar. 'I have the experience of working on the land of others. Handing in a half, third or fourth [of what I made].' His role in MST is at the heart of their education programme.

In the early days, children in the movement would recount teachers telling them that 'your parents are land thieves'. As the number of kids in MST grew, Edgar explained that the push for a strong education programme was led by the mothers of the movement who felt the need to help those children understand the situation and collective they were in. But it went beyond the education of youth. Given the low level of literacy in the rural areas, MST made a push to teach every person in the encampments and assentamentos to become literate. There was a recognition that the struggle for land and the nurturing of education are parallel.[24] Over the last three decades, the movement has taught 100,000 adults to read and write.[25]

While literacy was essential to the movement, it was just as vital to develop an educational programme that understands the political circumstances around them as opposed to what Edgar called a 'banking education'.

This term was coined by Brazilian educator Paulo Freire, a defining influence on Boal's work. In his book *Pedagogy of the Oppressed*, Freire described 'banking education' as the type that sees students as passive. One that sets the teacher as the active participant that bestows knowledge upon the students.

That banking education, he wrote, 'leads the students to memorise mechanically the narrated content. Worse yet, it turns them into "containers", into "receptacles" to be "filled" by the teacher [...] Education thus becomes an act of depositing.' In this system, education becomes a gift from those who have knowledge to 'those they consider to know nothing.'[26]

Freire proposed that teaching should not simply be this process of depositing information. Instead, it must awaken a curious approach to the systems that create the world surrounding the student. 'Only dialogue,' he affirmed, 'which requires critical thinking, is also capable of generating critical thinking. Without dialogue there is no communication and without communication there can be no education.'[27]

This critical thinking, in the context of MST, is a tool through which people see themselves within the scaffolding of power that surrounds them, and eventually dismantle it. It is an educational transformation into people who see themselves as agents in the future of their cause and, in Edgar's words, 'inheritors of the struggles that preceded us.'

While the educational push at MST was about literacy, an essential goal was to ask critical questions of the system that made them 'sem-terra' (the term that refers to the condition of being without land) in the first place. As Edgar put it during our interview, 'Education helps people understand themselves *inside* of history.' It must root a person into their community so they can grow as opposed to plucking them out. Building this sense of belonging in MST, of having a stake on the cause of land reform, becomes essential in collectivising their experience. Deeply informed by Freire's pedagogy, the movement's approach to education is about making the structures of power around their community known.

I asked him how change happens. He answered with a word that can't be easily interpreted: mística. It can be directly translated as 'mystics' but means something closer to 'sacraments'. He read the confusion in my face and explained that what he meant is the collection of memory, ancestry, symbols. Elements that 'create an identity'.

He told me about being sem-terra, the injustice that led to the formation of MST, but also being Sem Terra, capitalised and without a hyphen. The latter is a label of identity, denoting your belonging to the collective. Thorough organising and material wins have come to define MST but, to Edgar, they hold equal importance to the performance of these symbols. The method of organising would be less effective without mística, and vice versa. In the brilliant *Pedagogy of the Land*, Roseli Salete Caldart argues that thinking about the education of children in the movement cannot be considered merely an educational programme, it is *the whole* movement.[28] Their existence within encampments and assentamentos is an education itself. It's what roots them in a community so they can begin to question their place in the world.

You can see this education in the way MST was built. It adapted to different Brazilian states and their specific needs when it came to bringing about change.[29] Instead of a top down approach, the movement has an organised but adaptable structure which served to strengthen the whole and turned it into a durable and resilient organisation, one that is both critical of the systems surrounding it but also self-reflective. To Edgar, a movement has to 'protagonise the masses'. If a movement can do so flexibly, without becoming ephemeral, then it can last a long time.

Organising in a way that both achieved wins in its outward goal, but also fortified the group internally, means they are much more resilient in times of crisis.

'We suffered less in the pandemic,' he recounts, 'and in this current flood, because we have an organisation.'

As the deadly floods continue to cause destruction, Edgar tells me that the entire national movement is now focusing on helping families who lost everything, Sem Terra or not. A country-wide bank of donations has been organised to help them. The movement has set up community kitchens, purchased a boat to assist rescues, supported the production of clothes for women and children who lost everything, cleaned houses after the storm and established short-term health centres.[30]

Edgar explained that MST wants to show those families affected by the storm 'the solidarity and tenderness of the world.'

Free Travel

I was on my way to meet Pinar Aksu for another conversation. I could barely wait to ask her more about the free bus travel campaign given the developments since our first interview a few months ago. After their promises, the Scottish Government's policy to implement free bus travel for asylum seekers was abruptly reversed. A statement blamed 'very difficult decisions to deliver balanced and sustainable spending plans'.[31] We met at the Hillhead subway and walked over to the University of Glasgow, where she is studying for her PhD.

When she heard, Pinar was as shocked as everyone else. 'We were all raging because we were like, what the hell, this is such a small thing.'[32] The feeling of a rug-pull was so strong that everyone in the campaign jumped into action.

A wide coalition had come together around this issue. Community transport associations became unexpected allies. It was in their interest to get more people to take buses because increased usage invariably encourages maintenance and improvement of services – a cause they have always supported. Organisations like the Mental Health Foundation also supported the campaign, high-lighting the health benefits that accessible transport to nature, GP appointments and socialising opportunities can provide.[33] [34]

Another key partner in the area was Scottish Faith Action for Refugees, a group hosted by the Church of Scotland that includes the Muslim Council of Scotland, Scottish Council of Jewish Communities, Baha'i Community in Scotland and many others. They were keen to make sure anyone who wants can reach their place of worship. Pinar talked about her astonishment, saying 'they did amazingly, and they did a press release, they put it on their website. I was just like… that's such an unexpected ally, but they were really good. I didn't need to do anything because their chairperson went ahead and did interviews and said: *Scotland can do this basic thing*… I'm so thankful.'

Each partner in the Free Bus Travel campaign coalition saw the issues from their own specific angle, and all agreed on the solution. Politicians who had worked with these communities also helped. Following the parliamentary debate on whether to reinstate the promise in October 2024, MSPs received a barrage of emails from constituents. From human rights activists and health workers to trade unionists and church-goers, an influential coalition was built, and at its centre were the individuals most affected by the issue. Pinar concluded, 'Full credit goes to the people who are sharing their stories, their voices.'

A movement 'needs to be collective', Pinar explained. 'All movements need to be collective. If not, then it just can't happen.' While there are leaders in the movement, community organisations can develop the crucial collaborative strategies and that is when 'the good ideas come out.'

'That's what you need in the movement,' Pinar reflected. 'To remove yourself from the centre of it.' Within that centre, critical dialogue is needed. The ability to disagree and engage with other people, and find strategic common ground. Not every campaign or issue is as simple as going out to a protest.

After a few weeks of massive pressure from numerous sources, the Scottish Government re-committed to providing free bus travel for asylum seekers in Scotland.[35] The campaign worked. Change happened.

I asked Pinar, 'How does change happen?'

She immediately smiled and shook her head. 'Depends what we mean by change, doesn't it? Depends on the cause. What is change, Sam? You answer me, what is change?'

I told her I'm not the one being interviewed here and that I have already done some atoning for the title of the book in the introduction. She suggested that meaningful change takes years of speaking and listening to the community, arguing that there needs to be a process where the community asks, 'What are we wanting? What is stopping us? Critical questions like who is stopping us? What, who, why? What resources do we need?' She sometimes sees young activists running migration campaigns and disregarding the voices of older members of the community who have been through this before, 'and that for me is very insulting. They might be in their seventies, eighties. They might have made some mistakes. Fair enough. But nothing is perfect. Campaigns don't happen magically and everything goes smoothly. And you need to learn from them so that we can generate ideas. Maybe now, we can do something different.'

Change happens when a community builds the educational process of understanding where they are in dialogue, and imagining where they could be, going beyond 'the banking methods of education, from one head to another. You actually get people to participate.'

Another tool that facilitates this process is Forum Theatre, a branch of Boal's *Theatre of the Oppressed*, where participants enact a real-life scenario of injustice and try to find a solution as the play develops, but unlike Legislative Theatre, the point is to stay in the conversation, not necessarily draft policy.

Pinar will often deliver a workshop with a community group, engaging with a topic like immigration. Along with others she will perform a scene emulating how migrants are presented in the media. Once they do, the audience can jump in with interventions. There are no wrong answers.

She remembered doing one of these workshops just outside of Glasgow. The scene portrayed some of the difficult circumstances an asylum seeker may come across in Scotland. Then it was time for the audience to intervene. A hand shot up from the crowd and someone asked, 'Why do they not just go back?'

I imagine this question is tough to hear, layered with assumptions that would be uncomfortable to Pinar, but as the story went on she seemed thrilled by the question, describing it as 'nice and juicy'. She was energised by it, almost as if she was thankful to the person who asked.

After welcoming the audience's intervention, she asked, 'Should we create a scene of what happens when they go back?' The audience watched as the protagonist faced all of the grim consequences that might befall someone returning to the country they fled. The question turns to the audience: what should this person do? Inevitably they decided: move to a safe country. This is the moment Pinar labelled as 'a critical moment of reflection', when audiences enquire and engage with information given in good faith.

But isn't it difficult to engage with some of those opinions about migration? The public discourse has become so toxic, I asked Pinar if she doesn't get put off from going into spaces where she might experience that anger. 'Their community centres are shut, they're not getting appointments at NHS, they've got that anger in them,' Pinar responded. 'And then you have people who are maybe newcomers to the community, who literally just want to live a normal life. These two communities are turned against each other. It's easy to blame, to say that, *oh, these new refugees, it's their fault.'* She raised her hands towards me in a pleading gesture. 'And who benefits from this? The state loves it. It's their simple strategy.'

While politicians and the media seem to be constantly stoking the fires that turn communities against each other, that may not be the case in every instance. In *Hostile Environment*, Maya Goodfellow argues that anti-immigration 'can't always be passed off as a product of economic anxiety or material change.'[36] While expressing that the myths about immigrants must be challenged, she argues that 'the UK's sense of self can't be separated from centuries of colonial domination.'[37]

Pinar agreed that the racism is there and needs to be acknowledged. Some of the people she meets make it clear to her that they would not change their views and she has to ask herself, 'Am I spending my energy in the right place?', but she has also met people who are keen to learn. Though they've clearly been looking at social media too much, and hearing these opinions from people around them, when you get to have these honest and critical conversations, breakthroughs can happen.

The conflict that emerges is not a hurdle, but the very point of the exercise. 'I tried to organise to go into spaces where we might have conversations that we may not all agree on,' she shrugged, 'which for me is okay.'

The skill behind these engagements is much more complicated than going into a hostile room and having a free-for-all conversation. It requires Pinar to observe the participants closely and ask the right questions. 'I think I've got enough experience to facilitate that conversation in a meaningful way, not in a way that we shut each other's thoughts, but we actually critically think, talk about… *okay, you did an intervention. Why did you do this? How do you think it could have worked out?* And I think that's really important, and you need to do that. We want that meaningful, critical thinking. We need to do that.'

There are other types of collaborative performance, and in some circumstances theatre may not be the right tool, but whatever shape it takes the goal is to diffuse tensions and create a dialogue. 'Sometimes it's too serious and we need some fun even if it's just to break down some barriers,' Pinar concluded.

The idea that change comes as a splash, as a sudden moment of intense action that transforms everything, is one that springs from the comforting fantasy that all we need is a person to be at the right place and the right time. It invariably relies on a single individual and ends in disappointment and burnout, as communities feel disposable and their advocates move on. It stands in contrast to the much more difficult work of getting to know your neighbour and building strong coalitions. Meaningful transformation demands a collective construction. 'Change takes time,' Pinar said, 'and it needs patience, it needs mobilisation.'

She divides education into two types, one that is given by an individual, and the other from a community that asks the critical questions together. Real change 'doesn't happen overnight' and it can't just be project-based and professionalised. It needs to be the ongoing process of a community understanding their context, opportunities and power. It's not a relic to be passed around, it can only be found through collaboration.

The Free Bus Travel campaign was a hard-earned victory and exemplifies how communities can come together to change policy on a national level. However, getting there was also a rollercoaster, requiring the campaign to pause, reflect and redirect. It stands as an encapsulation of Pinar's approach – an action that collectively identified its target, shared responsibilities for its delivery and found unlikely allies without compromising its goal. It was created through constructive dialogue.

To end our conversation, I asked Pinar about this sense of overwhelming opposition. How can someone continue to feel motivated when the entire system seems so slow and reluctant to change? How can you not get overcome by anger and hopelessness?

'It's… I can't. We can't. That's what the system wants us to feel like. If we feel hopeless, we can't continue. You know what? I don't have time to be angry.'

Chapter 2
Agitate

In 2021, Tim Hewes woke up with one thing in mind: he was going to sew his own lips shut. The now-75-year-old priest had been planning this action for six months. There is a lot to consider when self-mutilating. Early on, Tim realised it would be difficult for viewers to see the thin, medical-standard suture material commonly used for stitches on camera, so instead he planned to thread the needle between his lips with thicker, waxed upholstery. A large folder carried all the necessary implements: scissors, in case of an emergency, and a mirror so he could see what he was doing to himself. He regularly takes aspirin but stopped a few days before the event so the bleeding wouldn't get out of control. He planned to stand outside the News Corp offices, which house the staff of *The Times* and *The Sun* among others, then perform the bloody scene as a symbol of the media's silence over the climate crisis.

Previously, he had been involved with Extinction Rebellion, Insulate Britain, Just Stop Oil and Christian Climate Action (CCA), a group of Christians engaging in non-violent direct action 'in the face of imminent and catastrophic anthropogenic climate breakdown'[1] which Tim has worked with the most. Even then, he told me that when he suggested the possibility of this action, the group was 'pretty horrified', but most of them came around slowly and eventually a few of them came along to help him.

The first time we spoke was on a video call.[2] The camera was pointing up, leaving part of his face off frame. Tim was previously a dentist for twenty-seven years and during that time he became an ordained Anglican priest, then worked in a non-paid capacity for twelve years. He has since retired from active ministry but is often still involved in church activities. After retirement he started participating in civil disobedience to draw attention to the climate crisis. He told me the act of self-mutilation was his most radical action to date.

This goal has never been more important. Since the Paris Agreement's target of keeping warming well below 2°C and pursue efforts to limit it at 1.5°C,[3] 2024 has been found to be the warmest year on record.[4] The UK Government's climate policy, which the CCA attempts to influence, is likely consistent with a 3°C increase in temperature.[5] I hoped that our conversation would shed some light on the strategy behind his activities and whether they can really shift the global picture. Do they have a genuine impact or do they just put people off?

One of his early actions happened when he joined a friend from the CCA at a hearing at the City of London Magistrates Court. He went as an advisor to Ben Buse, who had been charged with breaking Section 14 of the Public Order Act during an Extinction Rebellion protest in 2020. Once there, both men took out the glue they had secretly stashed (Tim's was in his shoe), glued themselves in place, and began live streaming. There was a rush from security to stop them. 'They're gluing themselves!' they shouted, but it all happened too fast. Tim's hand was affixed to the railings of the visitors' gallery while Ben stuck his hand to the wall.

Once they were attached, there was an annoyed awkwardness from the staff.

'Okay. Can you just turn it off, please?' They tried to ascertain what was happening and asked the protesters if they could remove themselves.

'No,' Tim said defiantly.

Ben began his prepared statement. 'Why are you prosecuting the protestors as the world is dying?'

A special de-bonding team that acts on occasions such as these across London had to be summoned. Once they arrived, the process of applying solvent to remove Tim's hand from the railings began. By the time they were finished and moved on to Ben, he lifted his hand and told the officers he only used a Pritt Stick. Both men were charged with contempt of court and sentenced to two weeks in prison.

On the call, Tim and I both laughed at the Pritt reveal, but the action seemed to hold an important place for him. It was emboldening to face these kinds of situations head-on. 'We shouldn't be afraid to do things that are gonna finish up with us in prison.' Early on, he considered that his position in the clergy might conflict with his new found pursuit. He went as far as suggesting he might need to hand back his 'permission to officiate' to his Bishop, who responded with an encouraging 'You keep it!'

Months later, Tim's hands shook in anticipation as the needle came close to his face. He wondered if he would be able to do it at all. But the moment his lower lip was pierced, he clicked into professional mode. It was like being in the clinic again. As a retired dentist, he had a clear picture of how the sewing would happen.

'I put the needle in one side.' He mimed a poke in the inner corner of his lower lip. 'Pull it out from underneath, put it in the top.' Once a thread was through both lips, he tied them together. They were regular stitches, the kind he felt confident doing for years. A repetitive process. In, out, in, out, cut, tie. Over and over again. 'But the waxed upholstery was quite thick so it was difficult to get it through the hole,' he laughed.

When it was all done, a striking image was left. In photographs from the day, Tim's lips look tightly sewn with marks of dried blood on them. He wore his dog collar and sewed patches on his shirt. One of which read 'MURDOCH DID THIS. MUTED CLIMATE SCIENCE' aimed at Rupert Murdoch's lack of climate crisis coverage across his media empire.[6]

He stood in the small pedestrian square between the News Building and the Shard. If you have ever been there, you know the area feels corporately desolate, like a privately owned concrete and glass villa with the echoing sound of cars and buses. People walking in and out were shocked as they caught sight of Tim. Some shouted 'wanker' when they passed the priest.

After a couple of hours, Tim cut off the threads, pulled them through and said, 'I'm done.'

They Call Me A Communist

These types of interventions have not, for the most part, been discussed favourably in opinion columns and news panels. Protesters in Britain have been enshrined as national characters through the early- to mid-2020s, and often derided in the media.

The UK Government has responded to the peaceful protests with increasingly draconian legislation, such as the Public Order Bill which extends the definition of serious disruption, makes its associated fines limitless, and increases law enforcement stop and search powers.[7]

On the one hand, these protest tactics have attracted groups of supporters across the country and, on the other, widespread criticism in the news. Very few active supporters of the cause have been above the age of 65.[8]

For Tim, the strategy behind non-violent direct action is to push politicians into action. 'That's what we were hoping to do with Insulate Britain and Just Stop Oil, to actually force the hand of the Government and companies to change their policy.' Ending new oil and gas licensing, and transitioning towards renewable energy in a fair and inclusive way, are among the policies advocated by Christian Climate Action.[9] He takes inspiration from historical groups who took similar routes like 'the Freedom Riders in the States and so on'.

One of the many lessons learned from historical examples of civil disobedience is that attention is the most valuable resource. In a piece by Social Change Lab,[10] Just Stop Oil activists described their early tactics as a non-violent assault on the capacities of the state, but no matter how many people showed up to a protest at an oil depot or Westminster, these actions couldn't gain a fraction of the attention that two activists throwing soup on a Van Gogh painting did. The constructive attention that may be brought to an issue, however, is often bad news for individual activists themselves. In July 2024, five Just Stop Oil campaigners were given sentences of four and five years for organising protests on the M25, the longest ever for non-violent protest in the UK.[11] Conspiracy charges are especially harsh and could result in anything up to a life sentence.

One of the opportunities to have an impact on the public debate was COP26, the United Nations Framework Convention on Climate Change, which happened in Glasgow in 2021. Tim, along with a group of Insulate Britain activists, staged a sit-in on the M25 ahead of the conference. Familiar to this kind of action, he knew police response could vary. Sometimes they have to wait for the de-bonding team. Other times, police officers decide to just rip their hands from the asphalt instead. Whatever came, Tim was feeling supported by the activists around him. While this act of civil disobedience was organised by Insulate Britain, many of the participants were from the Christian Climate Action group. 'Doing actions on your own is mind-bending,' he explained. 'Doing it in a group, we can actually support each other.'

The anticipation built as the group distributed orange vests on the hard shoulder. Cars zipped past honking their horns as the drivers realised what was about to happen. Among the group was Sue Parfitt, an eighty-two-year-old priest. She waited for a signal from a fellow protestor to walk to the middle of the M25. During the training sessions for the action, Sue was aware of the danger and a little scared. But now, standing here in the thick of it, she was ready to go ahead. They would usually wait for someone to walk out and stop the cars, sit down in a line, and block the traffic. This time, however, the group stopped the flow of vehicles together.

Sue felt quite numb, perhaps as a natural reaction to the nerves. They walked into traffic waving down cars so they would stop. A few drivers sped away quickly to avoid the blockage. She was accompanied by another activist, a woman twenty years her junior, who supports her in these types of actions.

'I'm not as mobile as I was…' Sue explained.[12]

I spoke to Sue in April 2024, three years after the motorway blockades. She recounted growing up under the fear of a seemingly impending nuclear war that motivated her to join peace movements. 'I think I come from a kind of people who are not prepared to put up with things if they can possibly see their way to change them.'

'When I was 18,' she remembered, 'I signed something called the Peace Pledge Union and I went out leafleting on an army base to get the recruits to leave the army. Of course, that was a very seditious thing to do.'

Her first time being arrested was during a protest at Hayford Military Base. 'The police came, and of course we were all chained-on in those days, there wasn't glue.' She had been less engaged in activism since those years but when her husband passed away in 2013, Sue found purpose in civil disobedience.

Out on the M25, as drivers shouted from their cars, Sue was thoroughly back in it. Receiving that level of animosity can be gruelling but in the middle of an action you get into a different headspace. 'You're always going to be next to somebody who loves you dearly and who believes in what you believe. You are probably holding their hand anyway, and holding the banner, and you just sort of go into a zombie mode.'

They sat down and focused in, making sure to allow ambulances to get through. One of the activists had the role of de-escalator. He walked between cars explaining what the action was about. Although the action itself doesn't aim to change the opinions of the immediate people around them, they've seen individuals change their minds right there on the spot, from frustration at the action into a sense of solidarity. In Sue's estimation, that has been happening more frequently as of late.

Sue retired as a family therapist and became a priest in 1994, one of the first women to be ordained in the Church of England. While spending time in Palestine, she found a library that held a copy of John Dear's *The Sacrament of Disobedience*. The book was formative for her. Later, as she was introduced to Christian Climate Action, Sue committed herself to non-violent protest. She has written extensively about her understanding of the value of civil disobedience. What is striking about chatting with her is how astute her courage seems to be. It's easy to imagine someone in her position naively walking into dangerous and uncertain situations. Sue, however, seems confident and clear-headed in what she would and might eventually have to give to the cause.

A few weeks after our initial conversation, a video of Sue pops up on one of my social media feeds.[13] In it she can be seen in the British Library with retired teacher Judy Bruce. They both made their way to the Magna Carta, a document from 1215 that binds the English King and the Government to the law of the land. It sits aside from the other exhibits in the Sir John Ritblat Gallery. There's usually a sombre reverence in the dimly lit corridors leading up to it. The further in you go, the quieter it gets. From their small handbags the activists produce a couple of comically oversized tools. While Sue gingerly holds a chisel, Judy hammers away at the outer glass. You can hear the faint shuffling of feet on the carpet. In the distance, an animation about the Cornish Rebellion plays on. Then, the sound of the octogenarians' peg crushing a glass surface. Once a visible crack appears, both activists step away.

'I am a Christian and I am compelled,' Sue attempts to speak over a security guard asking someone to stop filming, 'to do all that I can to alleviate the appalling suffering that is coming down the line and is here already. Whatever it takes.'

When we spoke a few months after the event, Sue told me that after the filming stopped, staff of the library came up to them with a friendly tone. 'Oh, there's hardly any damage. Just go, ladies. Leave now.'[14]

But the two activists insisted. 'You must call the police, say there's an incident in the treasury.'

Once the police arrived, they also encouraged the women to leave but again they insisted. 'We have caused criminal damage. You have to arrest us.'

It is in moments like this that demographic factors work in Sue's favour as everyone seems to extend more sympathy to the grey-haired 82-year-old than they might do young activists who are often brutalised in these contexts. She sees her age as an opportunity, not a hindrance, but these types of stories have much less impact without an arrest. Not being taken by police means it is more likely that this event won't make the news at all.

The video did reach the wide audience they hoped and they became the subjects of the national discourse at the time. John Woodcock, Lord Walney of the House of Lords, was interviewed soon after and expressed his worry about what might have happened 'if activists had got to the Magna Carta last week and managed to damage it in the name of climate change…'[15] Interviewer Jon Sopel quickly jumped in. 'Two women in their eighties?!' He equivocates in his response but eventually says that it's not okay to damage priceless artifacts 'in the name of whatever.' His suggestion for how change should happen comes down to 'try and change more people's minds', he paused, '…through elected politics.'

For a second, let's ignore the fact that the advice for activists to encourage change by voting came from a member of the, famously not-elected, House of Lords. The two protesters never intended to damage the Magna Carta and if you watch the video, you might ask yourself if they had the ability to do it at all. They cracked one of the protective layers and even then, only just. What they did intend to achieve was to create a shocking scene that would influence national debate.

I asked Sue about being in the eye of the storm of public discourse. She responded with a quote from the late Latin American Archbishop and Liberation Theology proponent, Dom Hélder Câmara, 'When I feed the poor they call me a saint. When I ask why they are poor they call me a communist.'

The leniency Sue can sometimes receive due to her age can extend to the courts but that's not always the case. Weeks after 2021's COP26, she was found in contempt of court for breaking a Government injunction in relation to Insulate Britain actions and ordered to pay £5,000. Before her sentencing, Sue read a statement in court which doubled as an opportunity to reaffirm the reasons for protesting:

'The Government's own Climate Change Committee announced on 2nd December – just 12 days ago – that if the Government sticks with its current policies, then it is helping to ensure that there will be a warming of the planet of 2.4°C by the end of the century. The Government is being criminally negligent and it is my duty to say so, whatever the cost to me…'[16]

At the end, instead of asking for the mercy that might have been afforded to older activists, she said, 'Please be assured that I shall continue in this path of civil disobedience.'

'It is of no consequence to me what you decide to do with me today,' she dared the judge. 'If you send me to prison, I shall use the time profitably to continue in whatever way I can, to sound the alarm about the emergency facing humanity. If you leave me at liberty I shall continue to protest in whatever way most dramatically draws attention to the appalling plight we are in, whether that involves breaking the law or not.'

Radical Flank

Undoubtedly, these actions have garnered significant public attention, as it is often their goal, but what does the attention mean? Keeping people who don't have any influence over fossil fuel production stuck in traffic for hours seems far from the process of persuasion needed for change.

There is no shortage of criticism for these disruptive actions. Some of it comes from the climate-denying commentators and politicians who speak of climate protests as they would of terrorism. But even for allies of the cause, a question arises around effectiveness. What could the fruits of this type of activism be other than putting people off? Are they moving individuals from neutral to opposition?

The responses I gathered from my conversations with activists are that this strategy is employed because of the 'Radical Flank Effect' (RFE). It suggests that the visible actions of a radical group will encourage support for more moderate groups, such as asking for more than wanted in a negotiation with the secret objective of settling at a lesser level of compromise.

I posed some of these questions to Sam Nadel, the Director of Social Change Lab which conducts research on protests and social movements. Asking how reliable the data around the RFE was, he told me that in national surveys, they have found that Just Stop Oil's disruptive campaigns on the M25 increased support for more moderate groups like Friends of the Earth.[17]

In 2022, Insulate Britain posted a statement declaring they were unable to meet their goals. 'We failed to move our irresponsible government to take meaningful action to prevent thousands of us from dying in our cold homes during the energy price crisis.' It reads, 'We have failed to make this heartless government put its people over profit and insulate our homes to do our part in lowering the UK's emissions.'[18] But Sam argues that despite the extensive criticism of Insulate Britain and other groups that use similar tactics, 'they had quite significant impacts on public awareness and public/political discourse, at the least, and arguably on policy.'[19]

Indeed, a 2024 study by Social Change Lab found evidence that the Insulate Britain campaign in 2021 was responsible for a meaningful increase of the topic in public discourse. The report argues that heightened visibility concurrent with greater parliamentary attention may have impacted the announcement of the £1 billion Great British Insulation Scheme. 'We would suggest an estimate based on 10% of policy attribution to Insulate Britain and 1 year of emission savings (in other words, a 10% chance that Insulate Britain sped up this policy package by 1 year) is realistic.'[20]

Radical Flank Effect is not, however, a silver bullet. There are case studies where it has backfired.[21] As Sam told me, he would not argue it is the most significant factor in disruptive and non-violent protests being effective but there is mounting evidence it exists and 'is one important contribution of radical groups'.

In many ways, RFE doesn't need to be a silver bullet. If that is the only strategy, the movement won't last. Sam continues, 'There is extensive research showing how grassroots movements struggle to maintain momentum over time due to resource challenges as well as the nature of protest-oriented activism that requires high levels of emotional and personal commitment, which can be hard to sustain.'

Bill Moyer's Movement Action Plan, created in 1987 and still relevant today, describes the eight stages social movements undergo. The framework explains how different roles must be played at different times for a movement to last, from start up to implementation. Civil disobedience is only part of a movement that needs to be long lasting and complex.[22]

Disruptive tactics are not meant to, in themselves, achieve all the demands within a given movement. The frustration with these tactics is often phrased through bewilderment at how sitting on the motorway or sewing lips could be possibly related to home insulation or climate change. Moyer's model, however, does not believe this stage shoulders the responsibility for an entire movement. Instead, they are only part of the beginning, the take-off.

When I asked Sue about effectiveness, the way she described her position in the wider movement bears out Bill Moyer's Movement Action Plan. To her, civil disobedience could have a meaningful impact but ultimately it is just part of what needs to be a variety of strategies in order to generate active change. 'I don't at all entertain the fantasy that me sitting on the motorway is going to change anything much,' she admitted, 'but I do believe that I'm a little bit of the mosaic of change.'

As Mark and Paul Engler describe in *This Is An Uprising,* 'Movements are primed to flare up when participants demonstrate the seriousness of their commitment.'[23] The authors explain: 'One main way of doing this is through showing a willingness to endure hardship, to face arrest, or even to risk physical harm in dramatising an injustice.'

While our conversation did not touch heavily on academic theories, Sue seemed to have an instinctive understanding that her part in the movement is about the 'flare up'. Perhaps that's the kind of lesson that decades of activism can teach – you're not *the* change, just part of it.

But she thinks civil disobedience has the potential to be a significant part of the process. 'If the whole church had sat down on the M25 motorway,' Sue posed, 'the government would have insulated the houses over-night, wouldn't they? There is a sense in which numbers do count in these respects. But otherwise, no, they are mainly symbolic.'

The sewing of the lips, from Tim's own admission, did not have the impact he hoped. At the time it didn't make the news and he wasn't arrested – two elements that would be key in generating those reverberating effects in the public discourse, though it did eventually get a lot of attention on social media and it often does the rounds again, years later.

From Tim's perspective, these actions are about moving the conversation forward and inspiring a moment of courage for observing individuals. Through the course of our first video call, he slowly showed more and more of his face on camera. By the end, he was fully in frame. He reached to the side and showed me a framed photo. 'My uncle was a soldier on D-Day. He lived his life courageously when he was a young man.' He tilted a photograph to avoid the glare of the computer. 'This is my opportunity to live courageously.'

He believes that if he can be courageous for an action, that moment may inspire someone else. On and on.

After a few meetings with these activists, I struggle to see them as ineffective or counterproductive. There is enough evidence to conclude their impact on how we talk about climate is both positive and non-negligible. Decisions such the early 2025 court ruling against the new Rosebank and Jackdaw oil and gas fields – whose consent was found to be granted unlawfully after pressure from campaigners[24] – may never have happened without the initial and ongoing burst of energy from the activists putting their bodies on the line.

I also can't see them as naive. In my conversations with Tim and Sue, what comes across is a motivation to make sure the cause is heard while they have time. They don't have the self-regard and importance that gets attached to some of the most crude stereotypes of climate protestors. Certainly, I can't say anyone who is engaging in making dramatic public statements is devoid of ego, but they are not out there building a personal brand. They are engaging in actions often at the cost of personal well-being. Sometimes those acts inspire, move the window of acceptable discussion in the country, instigate acts of courage.

They are regularly mangling their own bodies and compromising their own freedoms to speak about a truth that would be just as easy for them to politely ignore. This kind of language is often reserved for heroes, but they see themselves more as a trigger to something bigger than individuals. To them, the actions are closer to a kind of 'kindling for mass uprisings'.[25] While some are undertaken in a more individual way, it is in the role they play within the wider movement that I see a collectivist impulse. They are willing to do things that may hurt them but support the wider movement.

People like Tim have given everything for the belief that any single action could be part of the spark that energises other avenues of activism. He has now been charged with conspiracy after one of the peaceful actions on the M25. Like the sentences for Just Stop Oil protesters in late 2024, conspiracy could entail an extended prison term.

Their sacrifice is not happening in a vacuum. There is no inclination that the current draconian drive to arrest peaceful protesters will stop. In fact, the state responds to these elderly activists with brutal punishments. There is an ongoing discussion that needs to be had about strategy and effectiveness. That's also true of every other form of activism. Meanwhile, if the Government is reacting to calls for climate justice by threatening octogenarians with life imprisonment, is it not worth offering them a portion of the criticism we often give to protesters? The more these policing powers are extended and used to squash a wider range of causes, the more precarious the defence of 'why don't they just stop protesting like this?' will seem.

In the time I spent with them, I observed a willingness to put skin in the game, to get hurt for what they believe in, and receive unimaginable prison sentences for it. Tim repeatedly referenced these 'moments of courage', which to him are the real cogs of change. It obviously takes a fair amount of guts to lay down in busy motorway traffic, but there's another type of courage I see in their activism. To know that your action is only, as Sue told me, 'a branch in the tree of change' and still throw everything you have at it? That seems like real courage to me.

Conspiracy

I eventually went down to Oxford to visit Tim in person. We spoke about the impending trial in which he is charged for conspiracy.

'My wife and I are trying not to focus on that too much,' he told me. 'We're trying to live authentically, live courageously now and actually gather the goodness from time to time.'

Gathering goodness, to him, means spending time with family (Tim has four children and eleven grand-children). It also means exploring nature and listening to music. When we first spoke, he was looking forward to attending an upcoming gig by one of his favourite bands, Faithless. While he's on probation and awaiting trial, he's also led church services a few times. As far as he can tell, most people have not noticed the ankle tag.

As I write this chapter, I find myself feeling a familial affection towards Tim. While people on the outside, myself included, often interrogate the effectiveness of these actions, the question he is concerned with is if they are not detrimental and *could* be effective, why would you not do it?

You could look at this perspective as a prime example of individualism, of focusing on one person and what they will or won't do, but when you look at their protests in light of the wider movement, they are sacrificing the safety of those individuals in order to boost a series of safer actions to come.

Sometimes people will connect the dots between these activists and their religion and call them prophets. Both Sue and Tim seem kind of annoyed by it. We usually think of prophets as fortune-tellers, people who are here to warn us of doom, but in the tradition of Liberation Theology, prophets are meant to point to the flaws of society now and imagine what it could be instead.[26] That's how I ended up seeing these activists. They are loudly identifying the current issues I have gotten so good at avoiding, while painting the picture of a world where everyone could have the conviction to give their lives to the collective struggle for justice.

Christian Climate Action's members have grown close over the many years and actions. They have supported each other both in demonstrations and in times when individuals decided to step back. They are doing what they can, and holding each other's hands through it.

'I was just a dentist,' Tim reflects at the end of our conversation. 'All I could do was sew my lips up.'

Chapter 3
Organise

On the morning of May 12th, 2023, Nick Troy started his shift in the kitchen of the 13th Note bar in Glasgow. He kept distractedly glancing between the window and his watch in anticipation of what was about to happen.

The venue had become an important site of the local music scene since the opening in the '90s. You will often hear about visits by notorious bands like Green Day and Franz Ferdinand, but it was in the showcasing of smaller, up-and-coming acts that the venue-bar-restaurant became a staple for local music. On that Friday morning, twelve days after May Day, it was about to become the symbol of something else.

The lead up to this day was tense for Nick. Health and safety violations in the venue had made it uninhabitable for the workers. Many faced shocking levels of low pay, insecure contracts or no contracts at all.[1] Negotiations had stalled. The relationship between the staff and owner was at a standstill. Every new day brought with it the question – wouldn't it be easier to leave?

Something needed to change. A sit-in was organised to show the strength of support for the workers, who were now members of Unite Hospitality, a union of hospitality workers across the country who the owner refused to recognise. The staff themselves could not join the sit-in. All Nick could do, then, was wait for others to show up in large enough numbers so this would be a meaningful act. He waited in the hopes that enough people would feel a connection with the union members at 13th Note that they would choose to spend part of their day there.

The bar seated 50 people so he was concerned that even if a good showing of 40 people arrived, the place would still look roomy. In the end, Nick had little to worry about. Over a hundred people showed up and packed the entire space. 'It was really class,' he remembered.[2] 'Not all of them could come in the bar, most of them had to stay outside.'

Attended by trade union members from Unite and others from across the city as well as regular customers, it came as a surprise to most people there. The mixed group chanted, 'You might think it's all bravado, we won't eat your avocado.'[3]

Nick, now the chair of the Glasgow branch at Unite Hospitality, told me about the sit-in when we first met.

To him, that moment was a big perception shift. It showed him 'just how powerless the management were against the union.'

While the demonstration was a surprise, the issues that led the staff to this point were by no means rare in the sector. 'Every single hospitality venue I've worked in,' Nick told me, 'has been, to one extent or another, breaking the law. Whether that's breaking health and safety legislation, whether that's underpaying workers, whether that's workers not having a contract.' This contributes to a transient industry, filled with uncertainty where workers end up moving from job to job without security.

Unionising a workplace has become increasingly difficult over the last few decades in the UK. Legislation like The Employment Act (1980, 1982, 1988) and the Trade Union Act 2016 have slowly eroded the ways a union can organise and strike.[4] Bryan Simpson, Lead Organiser for Unite Hospitality, told me the sector has the highest rate of zero hour contracts in any in the UK.[5] According to research, 32% of its workforce is under insecure agreements.[6] He explained that 'it's a kind of toxic combination of precarity in terms of not knowing one week to the next, whether you're going to get shifts […] and the transient nature of it.' These elements make the hospitality industry notoriously difficult to unionise, and its workers vulnerable to unimaginable abuse by bosses.

Before Nick was in the middle of highly-visible union action at 13th Note, he already understood the impact that unionised workers can have. He grew up in East Kilbride, the same town where, in 1974, union workers in the Rolls Royce factory refused to work on jet engines bound to Augusto Pinochet's brutal rule in Chile. He draws inspiration from the trade unionists in his town. Writing about their achievement for *Tribune Magazine*, he explains that 'they proved to the world that acts of defiance can undermine a seemingly insurmountable enemy, while illuminating the material relationships that link workers and their interests everywhere.'[7]

To him, unions are how workers exert real power. Workers collectivising their issues is what leads to change: 'You will never, as an individual or as a collection of individuals, be able to halt production in an arms factory for four years the way Rolls Royce [workers] did.'

The Cost of a Pint

Around the age of eighteen, Nick frequented the Note with his girlfriend, but it wasn't until 2022 that he started working in the kitchen and experiencing the many issues surrounding the venue. The situation eventually deteriorated to a point where some of the workers enacted Section 44 of the Employment Act, which protects staff in cases where there is immediate health and safety risk.

Nick, already a union member, was convinced that the way to get better conditions was for his colleagues to join and negotiate together. He had come from a bad experience in a union-busting venue and knew that rallying others to join was an important step in this process. That work of persuasion, however, is not at all simple. The transient nature of the industry creates a high staff turnover which may mean that finding another job seems easier than sticking around in a tense and protracted dispute, and the bosses know this. Many even sweeten the deal by offering small perks, like free drinks, to keep everybody on side.

A couple of the staff, Brendan and Kay, were up for spearheading a unionising effort with Nick in the early days, so they listed each employee across the kitchen, venue and bar, and assigned a colour to every individual. Red for the ones who seemed openly unwilling to join a union, amber for the maybes, and green for the ones very much open to the idea. Once the map was laid out, it was time for the pitch.

Brendan Armstrong, one of the three organisers, was a 28-year-old chef at the Note who only joined the union when Nick started working in the kitchen. He first heard of the job when going to the venue to play Dungeons & Dragons with friends. He has been working or studying as a chef for the last fourteen years and, while he was not a union member back then, he was most definitely a 'green'. As conditions got worse in the venue – damp, mould, and now a rodent problem – he knew they needed to act.

When I asked him about what gave him the final motivation to join the union, he explained it was down to Nick's insistence. 'It was consistent,' he laughed. 'Whenever there was a complaint he was just like *You know, the union can help with that* then he was like *Have you guys joined a union yet?*[8]

'See, if it stops you coming in every day,' Brendan joked, 'I will join the union.' And join the union he did. But what had been a fruitful strategy within the confines of the kitchen was not quite as simple for the physically separate areas of the venue – where most of the reds and ambers were. The time they had available was limited, segregated to quiet hours on quiet days.

I asked Nick to give me the pitch as if I were working behind the bar. With no hesitation, he started.

'It costs us £1.50 for this pint of Innis & Gunn, right?'[9] He pointed at the imaginary tap. 'By the time that pint comes up through the pipes into a glass and is served, that's £5.50. So from £1.50 to £5.50. What is the process? And it may be an easy process, but that process is solely you being able to pour the pint. Know what I mean? And it's you facilitating it. You might say, *Oh anyone can pour a pint*, and that may be true, but you are the one doing it. You are the one behind it, doing it.

Selling your time and your energy. Selling your Friday and Saturday nights to do it.'

He admitted this is a bastardisation of Marx's labour theory of value, which highlights that value is created, primarily, by the labour which the worker has put into the product. The boss makes a profit when the worker creates more value than she is paid for that labour. Nonetheless, the pitch manages to successfully communicate the tension between the workers who bring the product to the point where it is sold, and how little of the money from that sale actually goes to them. You could do it with a pint of beer or, as Nick suggested, the ingredients of a salad. The principle is the same: the product is sold at these venues for a higher value than the sum of its parts, that value is imbued by the process performed by the bartenders and chefs, therefore their 'cut' for creating that value should be much higher.

Of course, some of the £4 of value created go towards equipment, electricity, etc... It's not just spare cash that could easily go towards salaries. It is easy, then, to label the workers as naive if they ask for any more of that money – it's 'bad business'. On the other hand, if a boss attempts to turn more of the £4 into profits by paying bad rates, over-working the staff and allowing disrepair, it gets labelled as 'good for business' and 'efficient'. When the squeeze comes from the boss, it's prudent. When it comes from the workers, it's unrealistic.

61

But Nick's point is that it is the workers who transform the space, the kegs of beer, the electricity running through the walls, into a product that someone is willing to purchase. If so much of the value created is a consequence of their activity, then the argument is that they should have more influence on how the value gets spent – even if not all of it goes directly into wages. Or, at the very least, it should be spent in a way that enables workers to do their jobs without fear for their safety and with access to a living wage. As opposed to all of those decisions being down to a boss who is so far from daily operations she later admitted to taking 'a back seat' over a years-long period leading up to the union effort.[10]

The pitch was successful because it dared to imagine a dynamic where hospitality work is given a small amount of recognition and control. Bar and kitchen staff are often vulnerable to some of the most prominent issues in Glasgow, mirroring many other cities in the UK: rising costs, sky-rocketing rent, unreliable public transport. In light of these issues, the £4 of value you create in every pint while facing serious workplace issues gains a lot more meaning. Accompanying the speech, Nick says, 'When you do have people's trust and people are convinced that you're actually looking out for them, then you can start to be like, *Stop complaining about your rent and do something about it.*'

Trust is a key part of it. In a largely non-unionised sector, there can be a lot of hesitation about rocking the boat in any way. When retribution for unionising efforts isn't clear and open, it can come in small ways like leaving names out of rotas. One of the reasons chefs are often in a better position for these drives is that the kitchen sets its own rota. The hesitation to accept a pitch like this is reasonable and building a sense of trust, essential.

The mapping of their workplace was a success. Everyone outside of management joined the union. The group was made up of 95% of the workers. It felt like they were fighting for something together against the tide of employers who hope their staff will just move on. The workers at the Note decided to stay with the problem, and the problem was about to get much bigger.

Diminishing Expectations

In 2021, Yana Petticrew was hired at Broadcast, a bar on Glasgow's Sauchiehall Street. The venue, much like 13th Note, was an important part of the local music scene. Yana herself frequented since 2017. 'It was where I made so many friends and, you know, really consolidated a lot of friendships.'[11]

She was already a member of Unite when she started working at Broadcast as a bartender, so when the staff discussed what they could do about issues in the venue, Yana knew where to direct them. Eventually, eleven workers in the bar (75% of the staff) signed a grievance that included demands of a full investigation into health and safety concerns, increased security in the premises, for all current and former staff to be paid outstanding wages, and more.[12] Unite also qualified the current issues at the venue as 'some of the worst breaches of health and safety we've ever dealt with'.[13]

Reflecting on what happened at Broadcast and the other examples of hospitality organising across the city, Yana told me how the demands are never as drastic as employers make them out to be. 'It's not asking for company cars or things like that, it's not asking for all these benefits and perks.' What they often ask for is fair contracts, working time regulations, sick pay, 'things that are just standard to the majority of people'. The fact that these basic demands are met with so much resistance contribute to this overall idea that hospitality is not a 'real job' and is undeserving of basic protections.

There seems to be a sense that hospitality workers can be easily thrown away and replaced. 'The industry itself is built on the fact that it's not organised and the fact that it doesn't have strong union representation,' Yana explained. 'The things that we thank the trade union movement for, such as the eight-hour day, the five day week… that doesn't happen in hospitality. Employers break employment law like that and they're fine with it. The second that you pull them up for it, the second that you say, actually, I'm not going to come in for a shift nine hours after I've finished, you're the problem, you're the issue because they'll find somebody that can do that.'

The more that the industry seems to devalue their labour, the more hospitality workers also see it as a transient job. Over the months of writing this book, I spoke to several workers in hospitality, all of whom confirmed this illusion addressed by Yana and other organisers. When faced with a specific workplace problem they will often say something to the effect of 'Well, I won't be working here for too long anyway', and while some of them do leave the industry altogether, many stay in this revolving door of jobs offering no security, safety and fair pay, hanging on the assumption that it is easier to move on than fixing what's happening here.

With little collective understanding of employment rights and diminishing expectations of a hospitality worker's worth, bosses regularly act outside the law. This dynamic has become so entrenched in the culture, staff are expected to see violations (working beyond reasonable hours, not getting breaks, etc) as a badge of honour. As legendary American organiser Jane McAlevey writes in *No Shortcuts: Organising for Power*, 'self-blame demobilises people, and it is a strategy.'[14]

And yet, hospitality is arguably a strong pillar of Glasgow's economy. In Yana's words, these spaces that are key for most forms of socialising in public – coffee shops, pubs, restaurants – 'don't materialise out of nothing'.

They take the hard labour of workers often facing conditions that have significant impacts on their health. By virtue of being important to the culture at large, hospitality is essential to other forms of activism. 'After these strikes, after these demonstrations, after these marches and things, what do you want to do? You want to go to the pub? You want to go and get a coffee?' The value of the industry easily overlaps with many other causes.

So, can change happen? Yana sometimes gets the feeling that it's not worth it. 'We're all lay members who are predominantly really skint,' she explained, 'and we're putting so much effort into this that it feels sometimes that nothing is shifting.'

Despite the precarity faced by so many hospitality workers, and the industry entrenched in a toxic culture operating against them, victories have been secured. In July 2022, a Broadcast representative stated it would 'close with immediate effect to carry out improvement works on the building and will reopen when all parties are satisfied that working conditions have improved. Urgent steps are also being taken to resolve the other issues raised by staff [...] Staff will be paid their wages during this time.'[15] The bar re-opened two weeks later.

To Yana, change becomes more likely with these kinds of public wins. 'It's about increasing the visibility.' As grim a place as the industry may be, she sees an opportunity in many employers being ignorant of employment law themselves. 'In other meetings that I've had with employers,' she recalls, 'you can see them visibly freaking out when you know what you're talking about.'

Now, as an industrial officer for the union branch, she speaks to a lot of workers who have watched what happened at places like Broadcast and been inspired to unionise their workplaces – including the Note. Her advice to them is that in an industry where employers are counting on you to avoid the hassle and move on, you have to 'stick at it'.

'You have to persevere through it,' Yana encourages. 'You have to be the member of staff that if people are having issues, they go to you to answer that.'

This rising tide in hospitality organising offers a glimmer of hope to other organisers in the city. For Yana, behind the movement is the workers' passion for what they do. 'People organise their workplaces and stick to this because they love those venues, they love what they do. I don't think anybody would go through the grievance procedure, would go through all of these negotiations, if they didn't love what these venues meant to them.'

The path towards these victories can meander where victories come with caveats. To some, becoming a known union organiser puts a target on their back, but Yana remembers that even in the most difficult days at Broadcast, the staff came together to run a bar that was important to so many people. They put in all this effort despite health hazards, lack of security and unstable pay.

In her experience, it's a simple equation. 'You are a worker producing profit for a company for somebody else. You should have a say in how and where that profit goes, what it does, and how you get treated.'

A Way of Life

Before the sit-in at the Note, negotiations with the employer were frustrating, often defensive and not constructive. However, refusing to budge, the unionised workers showed their strength in numbers after launching a collective grievance in February 2023. this led to some wins – assurances of a wage increase, the end of age discrimination in staff pay (while above the minimum wage, still below the national living wage[16]), and a kitchen refurbishment. The sit-in was a boost, but these promises never fully materialised. Staff received a grievance appeal from the owner stating the many safety issues had been fixed[17] though soon after, environmental health went in for a check and closed the venue with immediate effect.[18] Even after re-opening, the workers realised how many of the demands were not met.

Promises of change were made but the measures taken were insufficient. There were still serious health and safety issues and unfair pay that did not meet the living wage. As the staff met to discuss these issues, they saw little alternative.

One of Brendan's favourite memories from that time was when the staff voted on whether to go on strike or not. There hadn't been a bar strike in Scotland for over two decades.[19] He can picture the moment they counted the votes in favour and realised it would go ahead. He doesn't think they got to this point by chance. 'It was definitely like a slow burn.' It took time for that trust to be built so they could all take a leap of faith together.

In July 2023, the unionised workers informed the owner, Jacqueline Fennessy, of their intention to strike every weekend until August. National news outlets came down to shoot interviews and segments. 'We didn't speak to *The Sun*,' Nick explained, 'but we spoke to everyone else.' These moments when everyone's attention seems to be focusing on you can induce anxiety. Suddenly they were responsible for representing their cause. The young workers felt like they had jumped into the deep end.

'I'm not a good public speaker, but I can speak a wee bit, right? And I can bump my gums, definitely,' Nick recounts.

Brendan tells me that what sticks out from that time is that it was 'great to see people actually caring'. Immediately, they gained a surprising amount of support. Leading up to the strike, customers made a point of showing solidarity. They often spoke to wait staff about it and left high tips. On the day itself, supporters from all over the city came and joined them on the picket line. Cars drove past honking their horns and waving.

As we talked about these moments when everything changed, I askrf Nick the question about how change happens. Reflecting on that time in the Note, he said, 'It's collective'. A strategy you often see bosses deploy in these types of disputes is to appeal to individuals by offering a raise, a bonus, those free drinks I mentioned earlier. They attempt to appeal to individual needs, ambitions, and often, fears. If the workers can't see themselves from within this collective, it all falls apart. It's death by a thousand small, individual concessions.

'When you are able to build that united front,' Nick continued, 'it becomes the weakness of the employer. They don't know why people might feel interdependent and why that would be a good thing. They just simply cannot fathom it.'

The precarity of the industry and the decades-long assault on the ability of unions to have meaningful wins, makes it all the more likely that an offer of personal security feels preferable to the uncertainty of a strike. So, when workers tie their interests to the collective, bosses are at a loss. The mechanisms they use to apply pressure no longer function.

When bosses are confronted with this immovable force, they can choose to negotiate with their workers or raze everything to the ground. The latter is what happened at the Note. On the second weekend of strikes, the owner liquidated the venue. All employees were dismissed.[20]

Through a statement on their official Facebook page, Fennessy wrote a lengthy announcement. 'With the business driven to insolvency by Unite Hospitality, it is time for the 13th Note to sadly close its doors for the last time.'[21] It denied allegations of health and safety breaches and slammed the union.

This raises a question that I was keen to put to the organisers. What do they say to arguments that the organising ended up being detrimental to the venue and workers?

Fennessy's statement articulated bewilderment, 'why an organisation designed to protect the welfare of hospitality employees would choose to sabotage its own members' jobs with full knowledge of the impact their action would have, I will never know.'[22] Some of the responses to the strike echoed the sentiment. A few labelled it as harmful to business and growth in the city. An article from *The Times* hit at the union actions, quoting lecturer in entrepreneurship at University of Glasgow, Catherine Owen, who expressed confusion 'a number of recent actions by workers involving Unite Hospitality in Glasgow have resulted in unsurvivable disruption to businesses. Even when those businesses have raised wages and improved working conditions, actions are still continuing until the business has to go into liquidation.'[23]

In an interview at the time, Nick responded to the dismissal. 'We are rallying round to support one another but we all feel totally taken aback by this. We basically woke up to find out that our jobs had gone through reports in the press – it was a complete hammer blow.'[24]

'People don't know how they will pay their rent or bills and we are all deeply disappointed that we weren't properly consulted and sad that this has happened.' He explained, as they dealt with the aftermath of the situation. 'It's a very stressful time and we are furious at the lack of respect we've been shown.'[25]

Bryan echoed Nick's dismay in our interview. 'She just showed the real power of an employer,' he said matter-of-factly, 'which is just to pull the rug from underneath the workers.'

In the couple of conversations I had with Bryan, he told me about the ongoing battles across the country as he tries to organise in the hospitality sector. There seems to be a pattern in how hospitality bosses respond to unions – expecting workers to be thankful for their paltry gestures towards improvement and never questioning the surrounding conditions.

'I hate this kind of correlation,' he shakes his head in frustration, 'for having the privilege of a job that pays the minimum wage, workers should somehow look after the profits of the owner?'

Bryan explains he is not naive about what a business needs to survive. That's why bosses need to get around the negotiating table and find a path that works. In all the conversations and stories I heard from hospitality workers in the writing of this chapter, one thing has become abundantly clear: any hospitality workplaces where workers rely on the generosity of their bosses almost always get less than the bare minimum. As Jane McAlevey writes about organising in the United States, in *A Collective Bargain*, 'workers did not achieve access to quality health care, the right to retire and greater safety on the job [...] because some wealthy philanthropists donated money to a certain cause.'[26]

The sector is filled with pseudo-therapy, nice-guy, talk. Bosses publicly saying they are big lefties who love unions, while keeping their workers in a state of terror and ongoing risk. Owners trying to negotiate down their staff's wages while having a framed print of Jeremy Corbyn on their wall – something that has really happened. At the time of writing, a Glasgow cafe that has seemingly engaged in a public dispute with Unite posted a statement claiming working there 'is not a job, it's a way of life'.[27] This is not an uncommon statement in workplaces, but many bosses will proudly claim it all the while acting in ways they hope will (and here's another phrase I keep hearing) put the fear into people, essentially suggesting that if you organise with a union you won't get shifts. You won't get paid. The venue will close. Even suggesting improvements and changes is framed as an act of insurrection by employers.

The strike is a show of power. It cuts through false promises and a race to the bottom when it comes to basic working conditions. It reframes the narrative from one where every effort is owed to the bosses' interest, and workers should be thankful for miniscule concessions, to one where nothing gets done without the workers.

As Nick puts it, without the workers 'no pints are poured, no dish is made, not a beat of music is played.'[28] Some may see what happened to the Note as a defeat for the workers, but he sees it as an experience that will inform and energise future actions. There is time for reflecting on what happened and learning the lessons, but this is just the beginning for an increasingly unionised workforce.

'The alternative to unionisation campaigns is that there would have been a continuation of working conditions that were having dramatic effects on the health and economic wellbeing of the people that worked there,' he explained. 'Something had to give, and it unfortunately is now something our movement will have to learn from. As we continue to grow and develop, it will become much more difficult for owners to close venues in such a way.'

Though it all seemed over, even Fennessey's ability to liquidate without consequences ended up being an over-reach. The organisers made a tribunal claim against their former boss based on the dismissal of the entire team without notice. In April 2024, the tribunal ruled workers should be remunerated 90 days of pay.[29]

Striking the Rock

'We did all develop very tight bonds,' Nick reminisced about the experience. 'Particularly during that period in the run up to the strike.' There was a significant uptick in attendance at the union meetings in the Glasgow branch in the immediate aftermath. At the first meeting back, the room was so packed they ran out of chairs. This enthusiasm stayed consistent in the following months, leading to tribunal compensation to over one-hundred Virgin Hotels' workers.[30]

Bryan sees the Glasgow branch as being on an 'unchangeable upwards trajectory'.[31] Our last conversation happened days after the record-breaking storm Éowyn in early 2025, the weather event that led the MET Office to issue rare red warnings across many parts of the country. The winds brought with it hundreds of new members to Unite Hospitality. Many had been told to come into work under these dangerous conditions that the MET Office deemed a 'risk to life'. Shattering glass.

Flying debris. Compromised building infrastructure. There's no better union recruitment tool than bosses being willing to throw their staff in these environments. The most recent notable growth in membership prior to the storm was during the COVID-19 pandemic.

Following the court proceedings, the striking workers established the 13th Note Co-op and applied to take over the space from the council. Unfortunately, their bid was rejected.

The staff looked for work elsewhere. 'None of us are jobless,' Brendan said. 'We all managed to find work somewhere else.' Now, the group, many of whom just had their first experience of organising a workplace, are spread around several venues across the city – ready to organise them. 'I am now the "Nick". Anytime anything gets mentioned, [I say] *You should join the union and then we can work as a group.* So yeah… I guess this whole union stuff has just changed my complete outlook in most of the things that I do.'

In a pool of young workers where knowledge of employment law is rarified, staff that have the experience and knowledge that Brendan now has, become invaluable resources. I asked for an example of where this knowledge has come into play and he tells me about the 'clopen', where staff will sometimes be asked to do the last shift in one day and the very first on the next, to close the venue and then open it again, a close/open.

However, it is against the law for there to be anything less than eleven hours between shifts and it may seem small but being able to articulate to an employer that anything below eleven hours is illegal is a valuable skill.

Brendan doesn't see himself as an organiser. 'I'm the chef that people go to for advice,' always linking what's going on to the rights of the staff, often putting them directly in touch with Unite.

So, I asked Brendan, how does change happen?

'As soon as you said that,' he replies, 'I instantly thought of the water droplets on rocks.'

I've heard this kind of analogy before, where water dripping on rocks over decades or centuries can erode said rock, symbolising that small, frequent impacts can make long-lasting, permanent change. Brendan continued. 'Change happens, but it happens very slowly, and sometimes it happens without you really noticing it until the change already happened. So, like, you get one person, and then you get another person, and then you get another person.'

'Eventually people will...' He stopped for a second, as if about to correct himself. 'I wouldn't say it's like dominoes, I wouldn't say you knock one down and then everyone just follows.' The distinction, to him, seemed to be about the role of the individual. Describing change as a domino effect means each person individually takes a turn in the spotlight.

The water drop metaphor, on the other hand, highlights the side of collective action that is about knowing your target. Acting with each other. Striking the rock. Understanding who the collective is up against. In an industry that tries to convince workers their deteriorating conditions are even more than they deserve, it's vital they know where to hit and that they do it together.

'The problems you have aren't just you. We all have them and we can all work together to get the conditions better.'

Conclusion
A Lasting Collective

Towards the end of writing *How Does Change Happen?*, I found a strong urge to tie everything in a neat bow in the conclusion, yet the stories I observed seem to resist that much closure.

Here's an example of something I didn't tell you earlier. At the end of the previous chapter, Brendan shared an analogy of water drops hitting a rock and the consequential erosion, this much you know. What I've been hiding is that when we spoke about this, he had an actual place in mind.

'So, there's like a museum somewhere,' he started. 'It's got rocks with constant water drops on it for 50 years. You can see how much the rocks have changed over the years.'

I was interested in finding out more about this museum. It felt like the perfect image to paint at the end of the book. I looked it up and it turned out to be a Capilano Cliffwalk exhibition in North Vancouver, Canada. Picture three blocks of rock. A long copper-coloured metal bar is held over them by two columns. Above each individual rock there is a small plaque identifying how long water erosion has been affecting each rock. The first one fifteen years, then twenty-five, then fifty. But looking further into the exhibition, I started to have some doubts. A lot of people online seemed to think the erosion was fake. Obviously, the water drop system is man-made for the exhibition but many believed that the erosion on the rocks was also artificially created and not accurate to what it would have been if it occurred in nature. I still thought it was a good metaphor to conclude with, so, behaving like someone who did not have imminent deadlines to submit this book to my publisher, I started looking for geologists to find an answer.

I emailed a dozen geologists in Vancouver and every single one who replied explained that the exhibition does not seem accurate, saying that not only would it be difficult to predict what erosion would look like, but even a period of fifty years would not be enough to show it in any dramatic way. I cut my losses and removed that specific mention of the exhibition from the previous chapter.

When we look back at how change happens, there's a temptation to simplify, to talk about these movements in a conveniently tidy way. At the moment, everything in society feels so uncertain, our liberties, rights and security so at risk that we can't resist a pull towards uncomplicated stories of change. We construct emblems of change that are obvious, clear cut and, ultimately, artificial. In turn, that risks setting up an unrealistic expectation that everything can suddenly get better with a bit of hope and a slogan.

This impulse to look for clear cut tales of straightforward change happening quickly and effectively can be an individualising one. Over the last year I have been keenly aware of this longing for simplicity as a response to injustice. It often takes the shape of personal responsibility – *as long as you do something, that's what matters.* Consider Umbrella Man, the protester who found himself in the middle of the JFK assassination. He represents an anxiety I have felt acutely. *How can I make a difference? Am I doing enough? Am I able to change anything? How can I feel hope in a world that seems unconcerned with the injustices that matter most?*

The common thread in all of those questions is *me*. The source of the query becomes the focus. If we ask a self-centred question, we will get a self-centred answer. It contributes to an individualising narrative where change-making lies in the hands of individual heroes. If the question we keep asking of activism is how it can serve our personal needs and worries, what we will create is a mirror image of ourselves. Personalising the struggle for justice is a consumer model of change, the shadow of a system it attempts to overthrow. Going down this road can turn activism into a brand, a paper-thin veneer plastered for others to see. It's a perspective of change filtered through a primary concern of optics.

How do we fight this individualised approach to change? If I can draw any common theme from the time I spent writing this book, that answer is collectively. It is about building power with a resilient organisation of people who listen, support and strategise with each other.

We are increasingly turned away from our neighbours in a system that benefits from communities never being strong enough to fight back. In a piece for IRGAC, Firoozeh Farvardin and Gustavo Robles diagnosed the way neoliberalism has eroded a shared sense of community. 'Decades of deregulation, precarisation and the hollowing out of political democracy have resulted in a present in which people feel they have lost control over their own lives and projects.'[1] In this moment when people feel more isolated than ever, they argue, the far-right has swooped in with three fallacies: the scapegoating of minority communities, promising a return to an idealised past and glorifying ideals of individualistic possession. These are individualising but comforting fantasies. So, what can we offer in its place?

In a small group like Christian Climate Action I see a fight against this idealising of the past. The civil disobedience group led by an elderly generation speaks as a reminder that we should be reimagining the future. They have done so while maintaining a sense of accountability and mutual support. They plan actions together and support each other at trials. Most of all, they understand that they are the kindling of a larger movement.

In the campaigns for the rights of asylum seekers in Glasgow, I see a resistance to the rampant scapegoating of minority groups in a way that is rooted in community. Finding allies in unlikely spaces, building coalitions, bringing groups together through difficult and constructive conversations. Not seeing education as just the depositing of information, instead as a shared awareness. When you hear celebrities and public figures talk about encouraging conversations in communities, they often end up meaning that they hope people would be nice to each other. It's a stock answer, a centrist politician's tired mantra, to say that the country needs to 'come together'. A kind of dialogue that leads to centrist compromise. Instead, people like Pinar are making way for communities to do the hard work of testing their ideas, understanding shared experiences and influencing policy through a collective effort.

In the work of the hospitality organisers, I see pushback against the glorification of individual possession. It's not just because someone owns a venue they get to act in whatever way they like. Their ongoing work is to speak against that fallacy, even among their peers, and build a collective sense of solidarity. The union members I spoke to identified a need for building trust and connecting with the people around them on a real human level. Being the first empathetic ear when workers experience a variety of abuses. Communicating their worth, and the fact that together they are much stronger.

All three rely on community, on a collective of people who can build and fortify together. They are building these movements from the ground up, through their day-to-day lives. In *Abolish Rent*, this process is described 'as tree roots slowly break up the sidewalks that order the spaces where we live, we can cultivate our movement over time, through the patient, everyday activity of organising.'[2]

The process of creating meaningful change doesn't offer the simplicity we long for, quite the opposite. It's messy because it is primarily founded on community and working with people which is risky and sometimes disheartening. Everyone I spoke to in the movements profiled here, sees change as a lifelong commitment. There are wins, losses and regular moments of frustration. They are not simple because building life with others is not simple. While their larger goals and strategy are clearly defined, there are a million smaller considerations, decisions and sacrifices made day-to-day to navigate this process together.

In a recent blog, Sisters Uncut activist Shanice McBean summarises it perfectly: 'We need to return to coalitions, and creating physical spaces where people mix socially, across political and identitarian fractures. We need to orientate our liberation struggles to class and capitalism – not a reduction, but an orientation. We need to organise in ways that build towards mass participation, and give up the comforts of insular activist groups that double up as impenetrable social bubbles.'[3] The groups doing the meaningful and lasting work, show a long-term commitment to building organisations that understand their place in a movement, nurturing relationships and fortifying their structures.

Two storms have been described in this book. One in Scotland, which exposed several workplace abuses as hospitality workers were made to work in unsafe conditions. Another, much worse, in Rio Grande do Sul, which exacerbated existing inequalities of housing and land. Both Unite Hospitality and MST, two very different organisations, found themselves in a position of being prepared to help when those storms hit. This did not come about by luck. For years they had built a structure that was ready to act in dangerous occasions like these.

Building collective power is not very glamorous. Rarely Instagrammable. Much like the rock erosion exhibition, if it looks too simple, it might not be genuine.

While there's inspiration to be drawn from these groups, they often have to deal with failure, process criticism and reevaluate their strategies and goals. They have to deal with the messy nature of working with people. They are not the immaculate textbook example of an activist campaign because they have to do the demanding work of building movements with others. The word 'community' has taken a bit of a beating in recent years – it can be used to describe your group of mates or a YouTuber's fanbase – but in the context of these two storms, what I mean by 'community' is strong organisations. The slow nurturing of collective power.

The work of making change necessitates, before it even starts, the thoughtful act of looking around. Building a lasting collective with people who work in our work-places, live in our streets and face the daily injustices we're fighting against. In the words of American author and social activist Grace Lee Boggs, 'The most radical thing I ever did was stay put.'[4]

So, can *I* answer the question of how change happens? No. But I have no doubt *we* can.

References

Introduction: Umbrella Man

1   "Accidental assassin: JFK theory alleges Secret Service agent
    fumbled gun." *NBC News*, 21 November 2013. nbcnews.
    com/news/us-news/accidental-assassin-jfk-theory-alleges-
    secret-service-agent-fumbled-gun-flna2d11634276. Accessed
    11 March 2025.

2   "Umbrella Man" The New York Times, *YouTube,* 21 Novem-
    ber 2011. youtube.com/watch?v=-yznRGS9f-jI. Accessed 11
    March 2025.

3   "HSCA Hearings – Volume IV", *History Matters*. history-
    matters.com/archive/jfk/hsca/reportvols/vol4/html/HSCA_
    Vol4_0229a.htm. Accessed 28 February 2025.

4   "Pepsi Pulls Ad Depicting Police and Protesters" The Wall
    Street Journal, *YouTube,* 6 April 2017. youtube.com/
    watch?v=-ZADj7dysVM. Accessed 23 March 2025.

5   "From (Individual) Fears to (Collective) Cares." *International
    Research Group on Authoritarianism and Counter-Strategies*, 13
    March 2025. irgac.org/articles/from-individual-fears-to-
    collective-cares/. Accessed 23 March 2025.

6   Vincent Bevins, *If We Burn: The Mass Protest Decade and the
    Missing Revolution*. Wildfire, 2023. p. 3.

7   Ibid. p. 282.

8   Douglas Rushkoff, *Survival Of The Richest: Escape Fantasies of
    the Tech Billionaires*. Scribe Publications, 2022. p. 3.

9   Hayden White, *The Content of Form*. John Hopkins Univer-
    sity Press, 1990. p. 1.

Chapter 1: Educate

1   "Inquiry into police killing of man who stabbed six at hotel." *BBC News*, 21 June 2024. bbc.co.uk/news/articles/c2558q2keq8o. Accessed 28 February 2025.

2   Pinar Aksu, personal interview, 29 June 2024.

3   "Hundreds of asylum seekers still housed in hotels." Karin Goodwin, *The Ferret*, 3 April 2021. theferret.scot/hundreds-of-asylum-seekers-still-housed-in-hotels/. Accessed 28 February 2025.

4   "End Hotel Detention: Working to create positive changes in our communities." *Mary Hill Integration*. maryhillintegration.org.uk/end-hotel-detention/. Accessed 28 February 2025.

5   "INTERNATIONAL DAY OF THE GIRL! SPOTLIGHT: PINAR AKSU." Mia-lia Kiernan, *End Immigration Detention of Children*, 11 October 2017. endchilddetention.org/from-fences-to-freedom/international-day-girl-spotlight-pinar-aksu/. Accessed 28 February 2025.

6   "Voting rights campaign a success." Scottish Refugee Council, 29 September 2022. scottishrefugeecouncil.org.uk/voting-rights-campaign-a-success/. Accessed 28 February 2025.

7   "Maryhill Integration Network." scvo.scot/scottish-charity-awards/vote/2023/community-action/maryhill-integration-network. Accessed 28 February 2025.

8   "Lift the Ban." lifttheban.co.uk/. Accessed 28 February 2025.

9   "#EndHotelDetention in Scotland." justrightscotland.org.uk/get-involved/campaign/endhoteldetention-in-scotland/ Accessed 9 March 2025.

10 "Sunak and Starmer scrap over tax and immigration in heated first TV debate." Eleni Courea, Peter Walker, *The Guardian*, 4 June 2024. theguardian.com/politics/article/2024/jun/04/sunak-and-starmer-scrap-over-tax-and-immigration-in-heated-first-tv-debate. Accessed 28 February 2025.

11 "Starmer confirms Rwanda deportation plan 'dead'." Sam Francis, *BBC News*, 6 July 2024. bbc.co.uk/news/articles/cz9dn8erg3zo. Accessed 28 February 2025.

12 "Immigration detention centres to re-open in removals drive." Faye Brown, *Sky News*, 21 August 2024. news.sky.com/story/

immigration-detention-centres-to-re-open-in-removals-drive-13200380. Accessed 28 February 2025.

13   "A Brief Biography of Augusto Boal", Doug Paterson, *Pedagogy and Theatre of the Oppressed*, via the Wayback Machine. March 2009. web.archive.org/web/20090302151127/http://www.ptoweb.org/boal.html. Accessed 9 March 2025.

14   Augusto Boal, *Theatre of the Oppressed*. Theatre Communications Group, 1985. p. 122.

15   "Free bus travel for asylum seekers in Scotland 'from next year'." Jody Harrison, *The Herald*, 10 July 2024. heraldscotland.com/news/24443015.free-bus-travel-asylum-seekers-scotland-from-next-year/. Accessed 7 March 2025.

16   "Why free bus travel for asylum seekers matters." *Scottish Refugee Council*, 10 October 2024. scottishrefugeecouncil.org.uk/free-bus-travel/. Accessed 18 March 2025.

17   "Sobe para 183 número de vítimas após enchente no RS; 27 pessoas seguem desaparecidas." *g1*, 9 August 2024. g1.globo.com/rs/rio-grande-do-sul/noticia/2024/08/09/enchentes-rs-mortos-desaparecidos.ghtml. Accessed 7 March 2025.

18   Edgar Kolling, personal interview, 21 May 2024.

19   "Menos de 1% das propriedades agrícolas é dona de quase metade da área rural brasileira." *OXFAM*, 27 August 2019. oxfam.org.br/publicacao/menos-de-1-das-propriedades-agricolas-e-dona-de-quase-metade-da-area-rural-brasileira/. Accessed 7 March 2025.

20   "Art. 184 da Constituição Federal, de 1988." jusbrasil.com.br/topicos/10657347/artigo-184-da-constituicao-federal-de-1988. Accessed 7 March 2025.

21   "How movements can maintain their radical vision while winning practical reforms." Mark Engler, Paul Engler, *The Forge*, 10 May 2022. forgeorganizing.org/article/how-movements-can-maintain-their-radical-vision-while-winning-practical-reforms/. Accessed 23 March 2025.

22   "THE LANDLESS WORKERS' MOVEMENT IN BRAZIL DURING THE COVID-19 PANDEMIC: HOW A SOCIAL MOVEMENT FEEDS A NATION." *International Research Group on Authoritarianism and Counter-Strategies*, 31 October 2022. irgac.org/articles/the-landless-workers-move-

ment-in-brazil-during-the-covid-19-pandemic-how-a-social-movement-feeds-a-nation/. Accessed 18 March 2025.

23 “Sem Terra contam a história da primeira ocupação realizada pelo MST, há 30 anos.” MST, 30 October 2015. mst.org. br/2015/10/30/sem-terra-contam-a-historia-da-primeira-ocupacao-realizada-pelo-mst-ha-30-anos/. Accessed 11 March 2025.

24 “MST alfabetizou mais de 100 mil adultos com a EJA em todo país.” MST, 22 June 2023. mst.org.br/2023/06/22/a-partir-da-eja-mst-ja-alfabetizou-mais-de-100-mil-pessoas-no-pais/. Accessed 7 March 2025.

25 Ibid.

26 Paulo Freire, *Pedagogy of the Oppressed*. Bloomsbury, 2000. p. 45.

27 Ibid, p. 65.

28 Roseli Salete Caldart, *Pedagogia do Movimento Sem Terra*. Editora Vozes, 2000. p. 260.

29 Ibid, p. 84.

30 “AÇÕES DO MST DURANTE E APÓS AS ENCHENTES NO RIO GRANDE DO SUL.” MST – Movimento dos Trabalhadores Sem Terra, *Facebook*, 3 July 2024. facebook. com/MovimentoSemTerra/videos/a%C3%A7%C3%B5es-do-mst-durante-e-ap%C3%B3s-as-enchentes-no-rio-grande-do-sul/1127255345237098/. Accessed 7 March 2025.

31 “Scotland scraps free bus travel for asylum seekers.” *BBC News*, 19 August 2024. bbc.co.uk/news/articles/ cjw3n63ypjwo. Accessed 7 March 2025.

32 Pinar Aksu, personal interview, 17 January 2025.

33 “Transport and public mental health.” *Mental Health Foundation*. mentalhealth.org.uk/our-work/research/transport-and-public-mental-health. Accessed 7 March 2025.

34 “Nature and mental health: our policy perspective.” *Mental Health Foundation*. mentalhealth.org.uk/our-work/policy-and-advocacy/nature-and-mental-health-our-policy-perspective. Accessed 7 March 2025.

35 “Free asylum seeker bus travel scheme back by 2026 – Hyslop.” *BBC News*, 9 October 2024. bbc.co.uk/news/articles/c79nj1yxrq4o. Accessed 7 March 2025.

36   Maya Goodfellow, *Hostile Environment: How Immigrants Became Scapegoats*. Verso, 2020. p. 158.
37   Ibid, p. 202.

Chapter 2: Agitate

1   "CHRISTIAN CLIMATE ACTION", christianclimateaction.org/. Accessed 28 February 2025.
2   Tim Hewes, personal interview, 19 April 2024.
3   "The Paris Agreement." *United Nations Climate Change*. unfccc.int/process-and-meetings/the-paris-agreement. Accessed 23 March 2025.
4   "Copernicus: 2024 is the first year to exceed 1.5°C above pre-industrial level." *Copernicus*, 10 January 2025. climate.copernicus.eu/copernicus-2024-first-year-exceed-15degc-above-pre-industrial-level. Accessed 23 March 2025.
5   "United Kingdom" *Climate Action Tracker*. climateactiontracker.org/countries/uk/policies-action/ Accessed 23 March 2025.
6   "'Climate villain': scientists say Rupert Murdoch wielded his media empire to sow confusion and doubt." Graham Readfearn, Adam Morton, *The Guardian*, 23 September 2023. theguardian.com/media/2023/sep/23/rupert-murdoch-climate-change-denial. Accessed 28 February 2025.
7   "Public Order Bill: factsheet," gov.uk, 30 August 2023. gov.uk/government/publications/public-order-bill-overarching-documents/public-order-bill-factsheet. Accessed 28 February 2025.
8   "A New Climate Movement? Extinction Rebellion Activists in Profile." Clare Saunders, Brian Doherty, Graeme Hayes, *CUSP*, July 2020. publications.aston.ac.uk/id/eprint/41725/1/WP25_XR_report_final.pdf. Accessed 23 March 2025.
9   "JOIN US IN SAYING NO MORE OIL AND GAS" *Christian Climate Action*, 10 January 2025. christianclimateaction.org/2025/01/10/11411/. Accessed 23 March 2025.
10   "Just Stop Oil's strategy in their own words." Samuel Light, *Social Change Lab*, 17 November 2023. socialchangelab.org/

post/just-stop-oil-s-strategy-in-their-own-words. Accessed 28 February 2025.

11 "Five Just Stop Oil activists receive record sentences for planning to block M25." Damien Gayle, *The Guardian*, 18 July 2024. theguardian.com/environment/article/2024/jul/18/five-just-stop-oil-supporters-jailed-over-protest-that-blocked-m25. Accessed 28 February 2025.

12 Sue Parfitt, personal interview, 10 April 2024.

13 "Just Stop Oil protesters in their eighties target Magna Carta." The Times and the Sunday Times, *YouTube*, 10 May 2024. youtube.com/watch?v=HxIUW1fmLNo. Accessed 28 February 2025.

14 Sue Parfitt, personal interview, 9 October 2024.

15 ""You'd hope we'd lock up terrorists and *not* people protesting climate change, right?" "Well, Palestine Action, the damage they're doing and the way they're terrorising workers, we shouldn't be relaxed." @LordWalney wants tougher measures for protestors. @maitlis | @jonsopel." The News Agents, *X*, 15 May 2024, 5:45pm. x.com/TheNewsAgents/status/1790785462942277823. Accessed 28 February 2025.

16 "REVD DR SUE PARFITT'S COURT STATEMENT." *Christian Climate Action*, 15 December 2021. christianclimateaction.org/2021/12/15/revd-sue-parfitts-court-statement/. Accessed 28 February 2025.

17 "Radical climate protests linked to increases in public support for moderation organizations." Markus Ostarek, Brent Simpson, Cathy Rogers, James Ozden, *Nature Sustainability*, 21 October 2024. doi.org/10.1038/s41893-024-01444-1.

18 "STATEMENT FROM INSULATE BRITAIN: WE MUST ACKNOWLEDGE WE HAVE FAILED." *Insulate Britain Press*, 7 February 2022. insulatebritain.com/2022/02/07/statement-from-insulate-britain-we-must-acknowledge-we-have-failed/. Accessed 28 February 2025.

19 Sam Nadel, personal interview, January 2025.

20 "What was the impact of the Insulate Britain campaign?" James Ozden, *Social Change Lab*, 29 April 2024. socialchangelab.org/post/what-was-the-impact-of-the-insulate-britain-campaign. Accessed 28 February 2025.

21 "The activist's dilemma: Extreme protest actions reduce popular support for social movements." Feinberg, M., Willer, R., & Kovacheff, C. (2020). Journal of Personality and Social Psychology, 119(5), 1086–1111. doi.org/10.1037/pspi0000230.

22 "Surviving the Ups and Downs of Social Movements." Mark Engler, Paul Engler, *The Commons*, 2014. commonslibrary.org/surviving-the-ups-and-downs-of-social-movements/. Accessed 28 February 2025.

23 Mark Engler, Paul Engler, *This Is an Uprising: How Nonviolent Revolt Is Shaping the Twenty-First Century*. Bold Type Books, 2016. p. 148.

24 New oil and gas field consent was unlawful – judge." James Cook, *BBC News*, 30 January 2025. bbc.co.uk/news/articles/c3e1pw7npklo. Accessed 28 February 2025.

25 Mark Engler, Paul Engler, *This Is an Uprising: How Nonviolent Revolt Is Shaping the Twenty-First Century*. Bold Type Books, 2016. p. 148.

26 Tracy Rosenthal, Leonardo Vilchis, *Abolish Rent: How Tenants Can End the Housing Crisis*. Haymarket Books, 24 September 2024. p. 142.

Chapter 3: Organise

1 "13th Note Workers Are Not Defeated" | Nick Troy on Glasgow's Historic Bar Strike." Skotia, *YouTube*, 29 July 2024. youtube.com/watch?v=XIUh02eKEew. Accessed 7 March 2025.

2 Nick Troy, personal interview, 5 June 2024.

3 "13th Note Glasgow: Unions and activists stage pay demonstration." Gabriel McKay, Luke Chafer, *The Herald Scotland*, 12 May 2023. heraldscotland.com/life_style/food_and_drink/latest/23518030.13th-note-glasgow-unions-activists-stage-pay-demonstration/?1. Accessed 7 March 2025.

4 "How consecutive Conservative governments destroyed union rights – a timeline of the UK's anti-strike laws since the 1970s." Steven Daniels, *The Conversation*, 23 January 2023. theconversation.com/how-consecutive-conservative-

governments-destroyed-union-rights-a-timeline-of-the-uks-anti-strike-laws-since-the-1970s-198178. Accessed 11 March 2025.

5   Bryan Simpson, personal interview, 24 May 2024.

6   "Percentage of employees on zero-hours contracts UK 2024, by industry." D. Clark, *Statista*, 21 August 2024. statista. com/statistics/407833/share-zero-hour-contracts-industry/. Accessed 7 March 2025.

7   "Hands Across the Sea." Nick Troy, *Tribune*, 15 March 2024. tribunemag.co.uk/2024/03/hands-across-the-sea. Accessed 11 March 2025.

8   Brendan Armstrong, personal interview, 16 December 2024.

9   Nick Troy, personal interview, 30 July 2024.

10 "Sour note as bar blames 'bully' union for closure." Matilda Davies, *The Times*, 23 July 2023. thetimes.com/culture/ music/article/sour-note-as-bar-blames-bully-union-for-closure-9cqsq32tk. Accessed 18 March 2025.

11 Yana Petticrew, personal interview, 16 August 2024.

12 "A week ago, our members at @Broadcastgla (75% of all staff) sent a shocking collective grievance demanding action on an array of issues below. In that time signatories have been removed from the rota and told that they don't have a job anymore. This is trade union victimisation." Unite Hospitality, @FairHospitality, *X*, 11 July 2022. x.com/FairHospitality/ status/1546558149871779841. Accessed 7 March 2025.

13 "Staff at Glasgow bar Broadcast say safety complaints led to dismissal." Katy Scott, *BBC News*, 13 July 2022. bbc.co.uk/ news/uk-scotland-glasgow-west-62136459. Accessed 7 March 2025.

14 Jane F. McAlevey, *No Shortcuts: Organising for Power in the New Gilded Age*. Oxford University Press, 2018. p. 199.

15 "Glasgow bar Broadcast shuts for improvements after staff complaint." Katy Scott, *BBC News*, 14 July 2022. bbc.co.uk/news/ uk-scotland-glasgow-west-62163634. Accessed 7 March 2025.

16 "13th Note Workers Are Not Defeated" | Nick Troy on Glasgow's Historic Bar Strike." Skotia, *YouTube*, 29 July 2024. youtube.com/watch?v=XIUh02eKEew. Accessed 7 March 2025.

17 Ibid.

18 "Glasgow music venue 13th Note closed due to mouse infestation." Katy Scott, *BBC News*, 6 June 2023. bbc.co.uk/news/uk-scotland-glasgow-west-65823325. Accessed 7 March 2025.

19 "Glasgow bar staff strike at 13th Note Scotland's 'first in 20 years'." James Walker, *The National*, 14 July 2023. thenational.scot/news/23654667.glasgow-bar-staff-strike-13th-note-scotlands-first-20-years/. Accessed 11 March 2025.

20 "Workers at the 13th Note venue in Glasgow win employment tribunal." Katy Scott, *BBC News*, 16 April 2024. bbc.co.uk/news/uk-scotland-glasgow-west-68816851. Accessed 7 March 2025.

21 "Official 13th Note." facebook.com/official13thnote. Accessed 11 March 2025.

22 Ibid.

23 "Sour note as bar blames 'bully' union for closure." Matilda Davies, *The Times*, 23 July 2023. thetimes.com/culture/music/article/sour-note-as-bar-blames-bully-union-for-closure-9cqsq32tk. Accessed 18 March 2025.

24 "13th Note staff in Glasgow blast owner for handling of liquidation." Amanda Keenan, *Glasgow Times*, 19 July 2023. glasgowtimes.co.uk/news/23667017.13th-note-staff-glasgow-blast-owner-handling-liquidation/. Accessed 7 March 2025.

25 Ibid.

26 Jane F. McAlevey, *A Collective Bargain*. HarperCollins Publishers, 2019. p. 243

27 "Brooklyn Cafe." facebook.com/Brooklyn1931/?locale=en_GB. Accessed 18 March 2025.

28 "13th Note Workers Are Not Defeated" | Nick Troy on Glasgow's Historic Bar Strike." Skotia, *YouTube*, 29 July 2024. youtube.com/watch?v=XIUh02eKEew. Accessed 7 March 2025.

29 "Employment Tribunals (Scotland)" assets.publishing.service.gov.uk/media/6613b1152138738e3b031b15/Mr_N_G_Troy___Others-v-_Javacrest_Limited__In_Liquidation__-_4106816.2023_-_Rule_21.pdf. Accessed 11 March 2025.

30   "BREAKING Over 100 @Unitetheunion members at
      @virginhotels in Glasgow have *WON* their protective
      award at Tribunal. The Judge has awarded them maximum
      compensation. This comes after the workers organised and
      negotiated to win their unpaid wages, holidays and tips."
      Unite Hospitality, @FairHospitality, *X*, 29 August 2024.
      x.com/FairHospitality/status/1829097054003405067.
      Accessed 11 March 2025.
31   Bryan Simpson, personal interview, 31 January 2025.

Conclusion: A Lasting Collective

1   "From (Individual) Fears to (Collective) Cares." *International
      Research Group on Authoritarianism and Counter-Strategies*,
      13 March 2025. irgac.org/articles/from-individual-
      fears-to-collective-cares/. Accessed 23 March 2025.
2   Tracy Rosenthal, Leonardo Vilchis, *Abolish Rent: How Tenants
      Can End the Housing Crisis*. Haymarket Books, 24 September
      2024. p. 144.
3   "Left Wing Pitfalls: Against Neoliberal Identity Politics &
      Class Reductionism." Shanice McBean, On Revolution,
      Substack, 17 February 2025. onrevolution.substack.com/p/
      left-wing-pitfalls-against-neoliberal. Accessed 7 March 2025.
4   Tracy Rosenthal, Leonardo Vilchis, *Abolish Rent: How Tenants
      Can End the Housing Crisis*. Haymarket Books, 24 September
      2024. p. 115.

Acknowledgements

1   Angela Y Davis, *Freedom is a Constant Struggle: Ferguson, Pal-
      estine, and the Foundations of a movement*. Haymarket Book,
      2016. p. 145

Acknowledgements

This book could not have been written without the participation and generosity of a number of organisers and activists who generously shared so many experiences with me. Special thanks to Unite Hospitality, Maryhill Integration Network, Christian Climate Action, Movimento dos Trabalhadores Rurais Sem Terra and many others who did not make it to the final draft. I felt challenged and inspired by their insights, and deeply cherish the opportunity to explore the topic of change with them. Specifically, I want to thank Pinar Aksu, Bryan Simpson, Nick Troy, Yana Petticrew, Brendan Armstrong, Tim Hewes, Sue Parfitt and Ruth Jarman.

Huge thanks to friends who read drafts and offered thoughts on the ideas and conversations in the book. They include: Katherine Mackinnon, Eve Livingston, Katie Goh, Judy Gonçalves, and Julie Cumming. Also, William Swan-Nelson, who came up with a specific idea that shaped the final chapter. I am immensely grateful to

Dave Close, who has been an essential part of this whole process – from the very first pitch to the final drafts. This book wouldn't exist without him. Finally, I am thankful to Lia and Dráusio, who convinced me to learn English in the first place.

I deeply appreciate how Laura and Heather of 404 Ink have been supportive of the discovery process required to write this book. Not just when it comes to the time needed to understand the subject and meet interviewees, but also the process of self-discovery as a writer. Their thoughtful notes, edits and support during the more difficult parts have been an education for me.

While writing this book, much of my perspective was shaped by the writings of Paulo Freire, Jane McAlevey, Vincent Bevins, Tracy Rosenthal, Leonardo Vilchis, Mark Engler, Paul Engler and research by Social Change Lab. I constantly went back to the work of some of my life-long heroes of non-fiction like Janet Malcolm, Jon Ronson and Jon Krakauer, whose writing was a safe port in the more anxious seasons. I also found great sustenance in the music of the eternal Aretha Franklin and the films of Elaine May and Mike Leigh.

During this time I had the privilege of organising with Living Rent. Their ongoing work to bring people together and build a resilient movement has served as a massive inspiration. I've learned from their unwavering willingness to resist people and institutions who seem infinitely more powerful. Thanks to my fellow organisers Meadhbh, Joe, Robbie, Allison, Levi and everyone else organising in Govanhill. Also, a mention of my dear friend Eleni and the solidarity we've shared through the year.

As I finish this book in early 2025, when world events seems to be going down a somehow darker path, I keep thinking about the Angela Davis quote I've had sitting on my desk from the first day of writing this book: 'We will have to be willing to stand up and say no with our combined spirits, our collective intellects, and our many bodies.'[1]

About the Author

Sam Gonçalves is a Brazilian writer and documentary filmmaker, based in Glasgow. His work has appeared in *The National*, *Counterpoint*, and *The Skinny* and he publishes bi-monthly interviews on Everything Mixtape.

About the Inklings series

This book is part of 404 Ink's Inkling series which presents big ideas in pocket-sized books.

They are all available at 404ink.com/shop.

If you enjoyed this book, you may also enjoy these titles in the series:

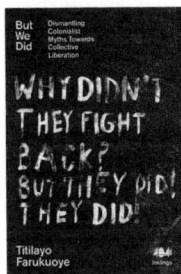

But We Did – Titilayo Farukuoye
School teaches us the myth of Black apathy, savagery, and helplessness, that slavery was inevitable, and that Black people have little power to resist and overcome its consequences. *But We Did* lays out this idea for what it is: a well-rehearsed lie exchanging snug high-fives with white supremacy.

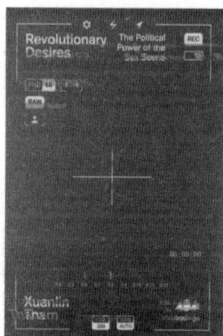

Revolutionary Desires – Xuanlin Tham

Cinema is becoming less and less sexy; yet more and more people are rallying against sex on screen. Why is the sex scene, demonised as it is, therefore more politically important and subversive than ever? *Revolutionary Desires* seeks to answer that question.

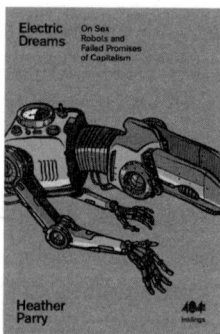

Electric Dreams – Heather Parry

Why are sex robots such a hot topic? *Electric Dreams* picks apart the forces that posit sex robots as either the solution to our problems or a real threat to human safety, and looks at what's being pushed aside for us to obsess about something that will never happen.